THE
NOT-SO-
COMPULSIVE
WOMAN

THE
NOT-SO-
COMPULSIVE
WOMAN

Sandra Simpson LeSourd

✓ chosen books

FLEMING H. REVELL COMPANY
TARRYTOWN, NEW YORK

Many of the names in this book have been changed to protect individual privacy.

Unless noted otherwise, Scripture quotations are from the New American Standard Bible, copyright © The Lockman Foundation 1960, 1962, 1963, 1968, 1971, 1972, 1973, 1975, 1977.

Scripture texts identified NIV are from the Holy Bible, New International Version, copyright © 1973, 1978, 1984 International Bible Society. Used by permission of Zondervan Bible Publishers.

Scripture quotations identified NKVJ are from The New King James Version. Copyright © 1979, 1980, 1982 Thomas Nelson, Inc., Publishers.

The quiz on page 46 from *Hope for the Perfectionist* by Dr. David Stoop is used by permission of Thomas Nelson Publishers.

Information on pages 85–86 from *Serenity: A Companion for Twelve-Step Recovery* is used by permission of Thomas Nelson Publishers.

Material on pages 102–103 is copyright © 1990 by Carolyn Wesson. Reprinted from the book *Women Who Shop Too Much* with permission from St. Martin's Press, Inc., New York.

The three steps on pages 152–153 are adapted from *Reclaiming the Inner Child* by John Bradshaw, copyright © 1990 by Jeremy P. Tarcher, Inc.

ISBN 0-8007-9201-7

A Chosen book
Copyright © 1992 by Sandra Simpson LeSourd

Chosen Books Publishing Company, Ltd.
Published by Fleming H. Revell Company
Tarrytown, New York
Printed in the United States of America

To
Len

With Special Thanks . . .

To all the members of my family for your love, encouragement, support and dedication.

To those people who write and telephone me and undergird me with their love and prayers; to my friends at the Catherine Marshall Center and the Billings Thursday morning prayer group; to Charlsie Byrd and countless others who have attended my workshops: my heartfelt thanks.

To Yvonne Burgan, Mary White, Elaine Brink, Pat Dowell, Virginia Payne and Ann Moran, who have contributed blood, sweat and tears to the production of this book. You're such blessings to my life!

To Drs. Neil Solomon and Richard Layton for your help and expertise in my physical recovery. You've been lifesavers!

And to those specialists for their editorial genius—Elizabeth Sherrill, Jane Campbell, Ann McMath and my husband, Len. You do make something beautiful out of my compulsive outpourings!

Contents

There's Healing in Art   11

1 Turning Point   15
  Recovery Principle #1: Seek Prayers of Others

2 The People-Pleasing Trap   23
  Recovery Principle #2: Say No

3 The Great Matchmaker   31
  Recovery Principle #3: Trust God's Love for You

4 The Perils of a Perfectionist   43
  Recovery Principle #4: Accept Yourself

5 I Won't Be Home for Dinner   51
  Recovery Principle #5: Smell the Flowers

6 How Can I Wash Her Feet If She's Wearing Pantyhose?   59
  Recovery Principle #6: Obey the Inner Voice

7 "I Never Was Pretty, But I Had Good Teeth"   67
  Recovery Principle #7: Give Yourself Away

8 "I'm Ready to Face 'Old Fang' "   75
Recovery Principle #8; Be Vulnerable

9 Broken Relationships   85
Recovery Principle #9: Be Reconciled

10 The Shopping High   99
Recovery Principle #10: Identify Your Real Needs

11 When Bed Was My Hiding Place   109
Recovery Principle #11: Expect the Best

12 Second Chance   119
Recovery Principle #12: Seize the Moment

13 Incest Comes Out of the Closet   127
Recovery Principle #13: Forgive Those Who Have Hurt You

14 The Conspiracy of Silence   139
Recovery Principle #14: Talk About It

15 Birthday Party Therapy   145
Recovery Principle #15: Celebrate

16 "Sandy, I Hated Your Book"   155
Recovery Principle #16: Be Honest

17 Letting the Tiger Out   161
Recovery Principle #17: Like Yourself

18 Learning to Say I'm Sorry   169
Recovery Principle #18: Confess Your Wrongdoing

19 Wounded in the Womb   179
Recovery Principle #19: You Are Loved! Believe It

20 I Blew Them All Kisses   187
Recovery Principle #20: Reach Out

When You Need Help . . .   196

There's Healing in Art

The drawings in this book are a joyous expression of my gratitude to God for sticking with me through much denial, anger and misbehavior. What talent I have with art was His gift to me at birth. It emerged during my early schooling, was shaped during two years at the Rhode Island School of Design and was put on display one summer when I did character sketches at Disneyland in California.

As this book began to take shape I felt an urge to depict some of the people and events: my children, Brad, Brent and Lisa; the tennis fiasco; Karen; my grandchildren's tea party; "Mother's Day Mary." Putting my experiences on paper stirred deep emotions; my tears often streaked the page. Likewise, drawing people I care about has in some strange way made me feel closer to them and deepened my own healing.

I believe God is using my words and drawings to pour out His love to them, and to the people—you!—reading this book.

Sandra Simpson LeSourd
Evergreen Farm
Lincoln, Virginia
April 19, 1992

THE
NOT-SO-
COMPULSIVE
WOMAN

— 1 —

Turning Point

ℛECOVERY ℒRINCIPLE # 1
Seek Prayers of Others

𝒯t is six A.M. and streaks of gray are breaking through the night's darkness. My husband, Len, is still sleeping. Quietly I slip out of bed and stand at the window, taking in the green lushness of this early morning in May 1991 at Evergreen Farm. Patches of yellow forsythia like bright sentinels line the driveway. Lilacs nod their fragrance from giant bushes swaying gently. Brilliant clumps of azaleas—fuschia, coral, lavender, magenta—dot the sweeping front lawn before me.

"Lord, You are indeed the Master Artist," I reflect. "How beautiful is Your world! How blessed I am!"

Suddenly tears sting my eyes. How this view contrasts with the view from another bedroom window thirteen years ago! As memories flood over me, my body begins to tremble. . . .

In August 1978 I was a patient in the Warm Springs, Montana, State Hospital. My weight hovered near 200. Totally defeated by addiction to alcohol and prescription drugs, I had attempted suicide a few weeks before, was rescued at the last moment by my daughter, Lisa, and put into this institution.

As one hopeless day slid into another, I had settled into a routine of sitting in my chair, staring vacantly through my dingy, nicotine-streaked window, chain-smoking three packages of cigarettes a day. At age 42, I felt my life was over.

I would have been surprised to learn that in my hometown of Billings, Montana, 150 miles away, a group of women were praying for me. These women met every Thursday in the Methodist church to intercede for hurting people. They kept a special file of desperate situations, which they labeled their "Ten Most Wanted List."

I was on that list.

Not being a believer in much of anything, I would probably have shrugged off their special request for me: "Lord, send someone to help Sandy!"

Yet this particular prayer was answered in a most unusual way. I told this story in *The Compulsive Woman*, but in the five years since that book was written, an element of mystery has been added.

The episode began when a nurse brought a new patient to the room that adjoined mine. My roommate, Jackie, and I were sitting on our beds waiting for the dinner bell to ring. We looked through the connecting door and saw a young woman collapsed on her newly assigned bed, sobbing and plucking at the covers.

Jackie and I looked at each other uneasily. A show of raw emotion was not uncommon in the hospital, but the moans of this poor girl were unnerving. "Oh, Jesus! Jesus! Jesus!" she intoned over and over.

"Karen, try to pull yourself together," the harried nurse was imploring. "It's almost dinnertime!"

"I don't want to eat, I want to die," came the muffled sobs.

Catching sight of Jackie and me, the nurse came to our doorway. "Karen is very upset. She was to be married next week and her fiance has been killed in a car wreck. Perhaps you two can speak with her and persuade her to come to dinner with the rest of the unit."

Jackie and I went reluctantly into Karen's room. I was repulsed by this new patient's religious wailings. "Jesus, help me!" she kept crying out. "Please, Jesus—help me!" She did not respond to our invitation to dinner.

When Jackie and I returned from the dining room, we were startled to discover Karen up and walking regally about the hall. The change in her appearance was startling. Her short auburn hair was combed neatly, framing an oval face. Huge, luminous brown eyes shone beneath thick lashes. She had changed into a long, white bathrobe and white slippers, giving her an angelic appearance as she glided down the hospital corridor.

I was struck by her loveliness—such a contrast with other disheveled, vacant-faced patients. But her constant calling on Jesus disturbed and frightened me.

The next day, alone in my room, I looked up to see Karen in the doorway.

"May I come in?" she asked shyly. "I'm scared of this place."

This was the first of endless visits to our room. Karen seemed to appear in a puff of smoke; suddenly she would just be there. It soon became apparent that she had appointed me her special friend and protector. I never had to guess who was behind me in the food line, her beautiful brown eyes searching for assurance. She would be waiting in the corridor when I left the shower room, by the door at the close of my therapy session.

One sultry July night, I tossed restlessly in the heat of the stuffy hospital room, listening to my roommate's deep, regular breathing in the bed next to mine. How could she sleep in this oven?

Suddenly I sensed another presence in the room. Half sitting up in bed, I saw a familiar figure. There was Karen standing in the doorway, her long, white nightgown startlingly bright in the moonlight.

As Karen approached my bed I could hear her crying. "Oh, Sandy, does Jesus love me? Does Jesus really love me?"

How to respond? Some instinct told me I had to comfort this weeping child. I got up gingerly, not sure how I could reassure anybody of anything. Awkwardly I gathered Karen in my arms and patted her damp hair. It had been a long time since I had held anyone to offer comfort. I had always been the one demanding attention.

Clearing my throat, I said, "Yes, Karen, Jesus loves you."

Her sobbing stopped in an instant.

My heart began to beat furiously. I felt cold and warm at the same time.

Karen detached herself from my embrace, wiped her eyes with the back of her hand, thanked me in a voice of childlike gratitude and slipped back to the adjoining room.

*   *   *

18

Now, thirteen years later, I marveled again at how that fragile event had begun a fundamental change in my life. What had happened?

The Billings women had prayed that God would send someone to me. I believe today that Karen was that God-sent person. My holding her in my arms, saying the words she needed to hear, had not only comforted her but had stirred something deep within me. In an instant I had changed from a totally self-centered individual to one with the tiny beginnings of a caring heart for others.

Not that in some supernatural way I suddenly became an others-centered person. That had to take place over a period of time. But there had been a supernatural change of attitude in my spirit.

Nor did I produce this change. It had come from outside myself. The only way I can explain it is that it resulted from the prayers of the Billings intercessors.

How did they pray for me?

As a group, I learned, they met Thursday mornings, began with songs of praise, then offered general prayers of thanksgiving for answers already received. Thanking God for His healing touch in the lives of their prayer subjects is crucially important, they had discovered, not only to open lines of communication with the heavenly Father, but also to lift and energize the spirits of the intercessors themselves.

They used Scripture prayer regularly, inserting my name into selected verses: "Strength and dignity are [Sandy's] clothing. . . . [Sandy] opens her mouth with wisdom, and the teaching of kindness is on her tongue. . . . Her children rise up and call her blessed . . ." (Proverbs 31:25, 26, 28).

Often the prayer went along this line: "God did not give [Sandy] a spirit of fear but of power and of love and of a sound mind" (2 Timothy 1:7). "And with His stripes [Sandy] is healed" (Isaiah 53:5). Over and over they prayed, "[Sandy] can do all things through Christ who strengthens [her]" (Philippians 4:13).

As I have learned more about prayer through my association with other intercessory prayer ministries, I understand more about the intense dedication and persistence and patience of those Billings intercessors. For years they prayed for me without seeing any results at all. When my life turned around dramatically and I began the long recovery process, they continued to intercede for me. They prayed specifically for God to send one of His emissaries across my path to help me. Karen was certainly that person.

How does prayer work?

There is a great element of mystery here, but we are told in Scripture that because Jesus lives forever, He has a permanent priesthood. . . . He lives to make intercession for us (see Hebrews 7:25).

Christ, therefore, is our chief Intercessor. He receives our prayers and lays them before the throne of God. To receive and handle these millions of prayer requests, God must have a tremendous heavenly communications network, a system that would make our most complex computer program look like a child's toy.

Also important: God's angelic help. "And the number of [angels] was ten thousand times ten thousand" (Revelation 5:11, KJV). That adds up to one hundred million angels ready to take action as God commands.

Seeing this picture helps me understand a little of how God can hear and answer the prayers of even a tiny child.

After publication of *The Compulsive Woman*, I set about making a list of the people I wanted to send gift books to. Countless people were used by God along the journey: family, friends, doctors, pastors, priests, counselors. But in thinking about those involved, I realized Karen and the Billings women probably topped the list.

We had no difficulty in getting books to the group in Billings—but how to track down Karen? I got off a letter to the Montana state institution with the dates when Karen and I had been patients, the ward we had been on and any other facts I could recall.

Several weeks later a letter arrived from the institution.

Dear Mrs. LeSourd:

Thank you for your inquiry. We have no record of the patient you mentioned in your letter.

My first reaction had been one of annoyance at their dismissive attitude. Then, as I reread the letter, absorbing the implications of its terse contents, my body was flooded with chills.

If there was no record of such a patient . . . could Karen have been . . . an angel? She had certainly looked like one. At times her physical beauty had taken my breath away.

But it was her love. Her grace. Her indefatigable pursuit of Jesus, and of me. A hound of heaven? . . .

I turned from the window to see that Len was awake and sitting up in bed. He looked at me quizzically.

"Memory time?"

I nodded. "I was thinking again about Karen. Could she really have been an angel?"

"If she isn't, Sandy, you'll hear from her. You've told the Karen story on national television, in your book, in articles, at dozens of conferences. Sooner or later, if she lives on this earth, she'll hear about your recovery and get in touch with you."

"Please don't use *recovery* that way."

"What way?"

"As if it were final and complete."

Len grinned at me. "O.K. You are in a recovering situation; you always will be. Recovery is a process that will go on until you die. How's that?"

"Much better."

As we began our morning prayer time together, I was overwhelmed with gratitude at how far on the recovery road I had traveled. But I wasn't kidding myself. I was still on a journey, along with millions of others, with much to deal with. One day I listed all the addictions I had been dependent on at some time in my life:

1) Alcohol and prescription drugs
2) Work, achievement and success
3) Money addictions, such as overspending
4) Control addictions, especially if they surfaced in personal, sexual, family and business relationships
5) Food addictions

6) Approval dependency (the need to please people)
7) Rescuing patterns toward others (codependency)
8) Dependency on toxic relationships (relationships that are damaging and hurtful)
9) Physical illness (hypochondria)
10) Exercise
11) Cosmetics, clothes, trying to look good on the outside
12) General perfectionism
13) Materialism
14) Tobacco
15) Television

Fortunately I could now cross out drugs, alcohol, smoking, hypochondria, exercise. Other addictions were pretty much under control, while food issues, shopping, perfectionism, people-pleasing and overspending were a continuous struggle.

But I was learning more and more how to build up my spiritual resources, how to deal with temptations when they assaulted me, and always how to keep my eyes on the One whose name Karen had called from the pit of despair.

–2–

The People-Pleasing Trap

$\mathcal{R}$ECOVERY $\mathcal{P}$RINCIPLE # 2
Say No

---

*T*he Karen experience began the healing process inside me. A few weeks later I was released from Montana State Hospital to go back to my family. But I was far from well. In June 1980 I spent 28 days at St. Mary's Rehabilitation Center in Minneapolis. After this came a period of six months at the nearby Jane Dickman Halfway House—all of this described in some detail in *The Compulsive Woman*.

It was at the halfway house that a staff counselor jolted me by saying, "Sandy, do you realize how male-dependent you are? Your thoughts, your actions, your needs are centered on men. You require their approval to be fulfilled."

"How can you say that?" I argued. "I've been hurt by men all my life."

The counselor tapped a paper on her desk. "The results of your psychological testing show you've been dependent on every man in your life. The problem with being male-dependent is that a woman ties all her feelings of self-worth onto what men think about her. You need to begin to become responsive to yourself and your own values."

She paused a moment. "Like most alcoholics, Sandy, you're a 'people-pleaser.' And the people you try hardest to please are men."

For several moments I was silent, devastated by this appraisal that I knew deep-down to be true.

"How do I get free?" I asked at last.

"For the next four weeks you will be on a male restriction program. This means you will not have anything to do with men. You can write or call one male member of your family once a week, but you're to avoid conversations with men, even eye contact with men on the street. You need to learn to trust women and the feedback they have for you."

At first this program seemed peculiar and unfair. It wasn't. I discovered how automatically I sought to make eye contact with men—in restaurants, at meetings, anywhere. Somehow the approval of these nameless males mattered. I would be buoyed by a flicker of interest, dejected by indifference. It was a searing discovery.

To break the cycle of male dependency, it was apparent that I needed to enhance my sense of self-worth completely apart from men. And, in fact, after the first few days of my male restriction program, it became a little easier. Each time I resisted looking at a man for approval represented a victory. My self-esteem was growing—in little flutters, but growing. By the end of the four weeks, I sensed a new strength in this area.

As I worked at relating to women, I became doubly aware of what a people-pleaser I really was. Especially with someone like Lauren, a younger dorm mate in the program. How she would rail at the "feelings group" we were all required to attend once a week. She would plop down into her chair muttering, "How I hate this place," and spend the meeting staring out the window, mindlessly twirling a long strand of her red hair in her fingers.

Many nights Lauren would tap on my door and want to talk. A life of wealth and privilege had not prepared her for the rigors of a regimented halfway house. She groused and wailed especially over being placed on a male restriction program.

"Oh, Sands," she gushed one night, "I know I'm not supposed to look at guys, but there's this adorable blonde lawyer I met at the treatment center who wants to see me. I don't know how his letter got through the gestapo at the front desk, but it did.''

"Lauren," I cautioned her, "you've already violated your male restriction by reading his letter at all.''

"Please don't tell on me, Sands. You're the only person around here I can trust. I really must see Mark, and I need you to cover for me.''

"Lauren, I don't *believe* you! If you're daydreaming about some guy, you're not working your program. You're just switching addictions from booze to men.''

Her lovely ivory complexion flushed a deep crimson. "Don't be like the old bags around here. I have this really deep need. Please help me.''

Sleep eluded me for many hours. Having been on male restriction for four weeks myself, I knew how valuable it was. I was learning to trust women with my feelings. This was a surprise and a delight since my female relationships had always been superficial and competitive. Would a conspiracy with Lauren now rob me of my serenity and deprive her of growth she desperately needed?

I should say no to her. But somehow I couldn't.

Lauren sought me out at the breakfast table. "I called Mark very late last night when everyone was asleep. He's agreed to meet me this afternoon when we go into town for our job interviews.''

"You'll never get away with this," I warned her.

She just smiled and tossed her mane of red hair into a swirling cloud about her shoulders.

And so I unwillingly became her partner-in-crime. On our job-hunting foray into nearby St. Paul, I fibbed to the counselors that she had been with me, that we had had lunch together and walked the pavements looking for work, even though I hated the deception. It chipped away at my self-worth, so fragile to begin with.

"Why do I let Lauren manipulate me like this?" I would rail at myself. "I know better.'' But the raging people-pleaser in me was still driving my bus, so I covered for Lauren whenever she slipped out to see Mark on the sly. Meanwhile, she continued to "play halfway house," plodding listlessly through the motions of our feelings meetings, counseling sessions and other required activities.

I wondered if others knew what was going on. The counselors were pros and would surely find out. Would I be unmasked as a confidante and enabler?

One night Lauren burst into my room to announce that Mark had asked her to marry him. "Oh, Sands, I love him so much. He wants me to meet his parents!"

I knew there was nothing I could do to dissuade this headstrong young woman; I saw myself in her, ten years earlier, as impetuous and bullheaded as she was now.

"No one can make me stay in this awful place," she continued. "I'll be gone before breakfast. Mark is picking me up. Thanks, Sands, for being my friend. Here—this is for you."

Lauren placed into my hand a small pewter figurine of a young girl in a swirling dress flying a kite.

"Mother sent it to me when I graduated from the treatment center. She thought it looked like me as a little girl on the beach at the Cape. 'You're free to fly,' her card said, 'unencumbered by the demons of alcohol.' She wouldn't mind my giving it to you—you're the one who helped me fly free from this place. Goodbye, Sands, I'll call you soon."

The door slammed shut behind her. I sat on the edge of my bed staring at the figurine, feeling miserable. I also sensed I would get caught for my role in this episode. The consequences would not be pleasant—and for Lauren they could be catastrophic.

Why was I such a people-pleaser? I knew better. *Honesty.* How tough that word was for me; how tough to walk it out as an addict whose life had been a mesh of lies. An honest person would have taken a stand, refused to go along.

The next morning the house was abuzz over Lauren's hasty departure. My worst fears were confirmed at breakfast.

Lauren's counselor, Robin, entered the dining room stone-faced.

"Lauren has left the program," she announced, "and I fear for her sobriety and her recovery. Even more disturbing are her plans to marry a young man she met in treatment. Neither of them has three months' sobriety.''

Then her blue eyes focused on me. "Sandy, I understand you knew about Lauren's male restriction violation from the beginning and covered for her. You have been the enabler, and by so acting you have not only jeopardized your friend's recovery, but you may have jeopardized her life.

"Enabling is a very serious thing, Sandy. The other counselors and I will decide on the appropriate disciplinary action to take in your case. . . .''

Having my male restriction program extended was painful, but much worse was the concern I felt for Lauren. Then, several months later, when I had completed my program and was working at the Minnesota Museum of Art in St. Paul, I got a call from Lauren. She and Mark had indeed gotten married and already she regretted it. Mark was drinking again, having an affair.

"Lauren, what are you doing for yourself? Are you going to your alcohol support group meetings?''

"Sure, Sands," she breathed into the phone, "I'm taking care of Number One.''

I suspected she was lying and also that she had been drinking.

Years later, still haunted by my guilty role in Lauren's tragedy— knowing that by trying to please her I had hurt her—I told Len the story. It resulted in a spirited discussion, not about male dependency (which, thank God, isn't much of a factor with me anymore), but about people-pleasing and the damage it does in other lives as well as our own.

"I still have trouble saying no," I conceded.

"Especially with your children," Len added.

"You have trouble saying no to anyone and everyone," I shot back.

Len looked rueful. "You have a point. We're both people-pleasers but in different ways.''

"How 'different'?''

"You became a people-pleaser as a little girl out of fear that others wouldn't like you if you didn't meet their expectations. I want people to like me, sure, but that isn't the reason it's hard for me to say no. I like to think of myself as able to solve any problem that comes along, especially in my work. To me a request is a challenge to my self-image. Saying yes is an ego thing.''

"How do people like us learn to say no?"

"Let's take a hypothetical case," Len suggested. "Let's say you get a phone call from a close friend asking to borrow $300. What do you say?''

This was hard for me. "I'd probably loan her the money," I said.

"Even though you know she can't or won't repay it, and will probably come back later with still another request for money?''

I squirmed. "If she was really hurting—yes. How would you handle it if it came from one of your close friends?''

Len thought a moment. "If we were really close, I guess I would tell my friend that I never made a decision on something like that without praying about it first.''

His eyes lit up. "That's it, Sandy! That's the way you and I should make every decision. Never agree to anything on the spur of the moment. Tell the person asking us to do something, or to give to a good cause, or whatever, that we'll pray about it and get back to him or her with an answer.''

"That sounds like a delaying action," I objected.

"Not at all. We pray for God's answer, not ours.''

"What if we get no answer?''

"Then we do nothing until we get an answer.''

I was not satisfied. "Let's go back to my friend on the phone. She's desperate. I tell her we'll pray about it. We do, but get no clear answer. So I tell her—what?''

"The truth—that we prayed and did not get the green light to loan her the money. We're sorry.''

"She'll probably think we're just using prayer as an excuse to say no.''

"She may. And she may be angry with you for saying no. But you're missing the real point here, Sandy. When we go to the Lord in prayer, we don't know what the answer will be. It could be yes or no. Or not yet. But the key is this—*we go to Him in faith.*''

A few weeks after this discussion Len and I had a chance to put this new approach into action. I had been letting myself get stressed out by taking on too many speaking engagements. The call came one night from my good friend Sherry.

"Sandy, the women of our church are having a retreat the first weekend of next October. Will you be our speaker?"

"Let me check my schedule," I answered.

That particular weekend was free, and I started to give her a quick yes. But I did have several other major engagements that month. Then I remembered Len's and my discussion.

"Sherry, there are some complications. Let me get back to you."

Len and I talked it over, then prayed about it. I wanted to do it for Sherry, but had a slight check in my spirit. The next day the inner check was stronger in both of us.

My no to Sherry did not please her, but it was a small victory for me. Nor did my friendship with Sherry suffer. I came up with the name of someone free to do the speaking and who turned out to be just the right person for that particular women's group.

I was learning. The Lauren episode was a watershed experience. It showed me the weakness of people-pleasing, that giving in to Lauren's demands had not been being a good friend to her. As a good friend I wanted the best for her. What was best for Lauren? To stay with the treatment program because she wasn't ready to be a healthy, responsible wife and mother.

It may be that saying no would not have stopped Lauren from fleeing the halfway house to an ill-advised marriage; but then again, it might have. She would have been angry with me, called me names and I would have felt bad. But if I had said no lovingly, she would still have wanted my friendship. She would have needed my friendship and probably would have respected me more.

As I have thought and prayed about the weakness of being a people-pleaser and the strength of saying no, I suggest these guidelines when you are faced with a Lauren kind of situation:

1) Pray about your response, seeking God's direction. Ask Him, "Am I doing this because it's the right thing to do?"
2) If saying no is your inner conviction, do it gently, lovingly, but firmly.
3) Be prepared for a negative or even angry response, keeping in mind that your no is actually a positive response because you are overcoming a people-pleasing weakness and are thinking of what is right in the situation.
4) If possible, follow up your no with helpful suggestions and loving concern for the other person.

More often than not, saying no will benefit both parties. The person saying no will experience an inner strengthening of his or her self-worth. The person refused will often discover in time that this was not a rejection, but for his or her own good and growth. And God will have His way in the situation.

—3—

The Great Matchmaker

$\mathcal{R}$ECOVERY $\mathcal{P}$RINCIPLE # 3
Trust God's Love for You

$\mathcal{M}$y six months at the halfway house marked a crucial stage in my recovery. For one thing, I saw clearly for the very first time that I could not for the rest of my life take even one drink of alcohol. For me, that first drink would lead to many, then to bondage. Even death.

Male dependence, however, was more subtle and therefore harder to deal with. I could look back over my life and see a painful pattern: the breakup of my parents' marriage, which I blamed (perhaps unfairly) on my father, then two failed marriages of my own.

For years drinking had helped to anesthetize my feelings of defeat as a wife and mother. But sobriety, plus therapy, forced me to a realistic appraisal of the liabilities I had brought to marriage. The following became clear:

My immaturity
Gamesmanship with men (based on deception)
Fear of intimacy
Fear of responsibility
Inability to share my feelings at a meaningful level
Selfishness

My turning point experience with Karen had begun to work on my basic selfishness. At the halfway house the teaching on male dependency convinced me that a lot more had to change inside me before I should even think about marrying again. And Lauren's disastrous experience convinced me that no male relationships were better than bad ones. I was learning that I didn't have to have a man in my life to feel worthwhile. That was progress!

Deep down inside me was the desire to be, at last, a real wife to someone. But I was learning to turn this area of my life, like all the rest, over to the "Higher Power" of twelve-step programs. Especially helpful was a short essay, "His Plan for Your Mate," given to me at a singles' meeting. Here are excerpts:

> Everyone longs to give him or herself completely to someone—to have a deep soul relationship with another, to be loved thoroughly and exclusively. But God says to the Christian, "Not until you discover that only in Me is real satisfaction will you be capable of the perfect human relationship that I have planned for you. . . .
>
> "Don't be anxious. Don't worry. Don't look around at the things others have. . . . You just keep looking up to Me, or you will miss what I want to show you. . . .
>
> "And when you're ready, I'll surprise you with a love far more wonderful than any you would ever dream of. . . ."

These words became guidelines. When on a Sunday night in March 1980 I made a total surrender of my life to God, I felt that if it were just He and I for the rest of my life, that would be O.K. with me. Perhaps I was called to be single. Perhaps to work with other single women, especially women addicts.

Often I would slip into an open church for prayer, such as Billings' St. Patrick's Cathedral where I would kneel up front before the crucifix. I found much comfort in this cool, darkened sanctuary. The hushed holiness washed over me and bathed my wounds. The Lord was indeed a husband to me as He promised in Isaiah 54.

I didn't need or want a man in my life at that time. I wasn't healed enough to have a healthy, meaningful relationship with any male.

Yet one morning as I was taking my brisk two-mile walk by the rimrocks, I found myself praying this prayer: "Thank You, Lord, for the relationship You and I have together. It's all I need. Yet I'm aware it could be Your plan for me to share my life with a special man You have picked out for me.

"If so, Lord, hold him close and meet his needs today. Bless him. Heal him. Draw him closer to You. . . ."

The months passed. My three children were in their early twenties now, grateful for a sober mother but cautious, clearly afraid I would go off the deep end again, adding to the hurts of past years. I ached for them, wept inconsolably at night over the damage I had done to them and so many other people.

Perhaps out of this sense of indebtedness, I determined to help hurting people wherever I could. I began to speak out more in alcoholic support groups. As I began telling my story here and there, a publisher contacted me and suggested I write a book. Though my embryonic self-confidence quailed at such a thought, I borrowed a typewriter and spent long, frustrating hours in front of it.

The result was a most unusual-looking manuscript. Someone advised me to keep a small spiral notebook tucked into my purse for jotting down ideas. Naturally I carried this idea to extremes! I scribbled ideas on anything handy—matchbook covers, paper napkins, brown paper bags, envelope flaps—then assembled these various remnants and stapled them to blank sheets of paper. These were interspersed among my pages of typed notes.

The total package was large, lumpy and unwieldy, with napkins and matchbook covers jutting out from all sides—more like something destined for the trash compactor than for the scrutiny of Ken Petersen, the Tyndale editor I was to meet with at the *Decision* Magazine Writers Workshop in St. Paul, Minnesota.

Something had to be done to transform the tottering tower of papers before me into something more presentable for my appointment. What could I do to make it more attractive? My eyes spied a yard of kelly green polka dot ribbon. Just what I needed for dramatic effect! Excitedly I bound my manuscript with the colorful ribbon, topping it with an elaborate bow.

The interview took place on the first day of my arrival in St. Paul. Ken was warm and friendly as he extended his hand in greeting. Why had I feared this man?

"You have a manuscript to show me, perhaps?"

Nervously I drew my creation from the depths of my shoulder bag and thrust it across the table into Ken's waiting hands. My beautiful bow drooped pitifully, mashed during the long flight from my new home in Vermont.

Ken's handsome face crinkled into a smile. I marvel now at his equanimity faced with such a hodgepodge of material. He stroked the ruffled edges of my offering thoughtfully, then untied the bow and leafed through the pages, making suggestions on the development of the material.

Elated at being treated like an actual writer, I pored over the week's schedule, deciding what classes to attend. On Monday afternoon I decided to attend a talk on creative ideas by a longtime *Guideposts* editor named Leonard LeSourd.

In *The Compulsive Woman* I told briefly how Len and I met at this workshop and the courtship that followed. Here is the story in more detail.

I arrived at the auditorium that afternoon early and found a seat directly in front of the speaker's podium. Soon I was joined by a pretty brunette from Watford City, North Dakota, who introduced herself as Polly Damaska. Her husband pastored a church and she had always wanted to write more than church bulletins.

She grabbed my arm. "That must be Leonard LeSourd now. He was married to Catherine Marshall, you know. He must miss her terribly since her death."

As the attractive gray-haired man stepped up to the podium, something inexplicable happened. A voice inside me said, *There he is.*

Excuse me, Lord, I thought. *Is this You? Are You telling me this is the man I've been praying for for so long?*

Impossible! I was imagining things.

Len finished his talk and gathered up his notes as the applause broke the quiet of the large lecture hall. I sat there strangely paralyzed.

Polly broke my trance with an insistent tap on my shoulder, her eyes wide with wonder. "Sandy, the Lord has something very special for you and Leonard LeSourd."

I blinked in amazement at hearing my own thought in the mouth of this total stranger.

As she joined the others gathered about Len, asking questions, I felt a sudden shyness, almost as if I were still on the male restriction program, and walked out of the lecture hall.

Entering the front door of the college cafeteria that night for dinner, I heard my name: "Sandy, come over here!" It was Fred Bauer, a former editor at *Guideposts* magazine whom I had met that afternoon. With him was Len LeSourd. Fred introduced us and Len and I sat next to each other at dinner, then again at the auditorium, where I found myself telling him of my long struggle with alcoholism.

To my surprise, tears formed in his slate-blue eyes. "I have a niece struggling with that problem," he said. "Would you be willing to write to her?"

He gave me her address and asked for mine. Noting that I lived in Vermont, he mentioned that he would be driving through New England later that month. "I'll give you a call."

It's the sort of thing people say. But sure enough, three weeks later my telephone rang. Len was in the area; could I make a room reservation for him somewhere nearby for Saturday night?

He had become such a workaholic since Catherine's death, he explained, that his children had needled him into taking this vacation trip through New England. "I'm supposed to stop regularly and smell the flowers."

I took that as a personal challenge. I reserved a room at the Montpelier Tavern Inn, a historic spot where stagecoaches used to stop. Then Margaret Guilmette, a creative friend of mine, and I went to work. Saturday morning we filled his room with the largest bouquet of flowers we could get through the door. Was my compulsive nature showing?

Across the top of the drapes that framed a large picture window, Margaret and I pinned a newsprint banner, *Welcome to Montpelier, Len!* Onto one of the twin beds we placed a cuddly black teddy bear, decked out in a hat trimmed with violets. Nestled next to the bear was a straw basket labeled *First Aid Kit for the Weary Traveler.* In it we put a box of Vermont maple candy, a clump of red grapes, crackers and cheese, assorted newspapers and magazines and a bottle of aspirin.

Finally Margaret and I taped Scripture posters to the wallpaper: *Our God Reigns* and *Let Everything that Has Breath Praise the Lord!* We giggled aloud imagining what the maid would make of our redecorating efforts.

Late in the afternoon the telephone rang. Len was chuckling. "There seems to be a bear in my room."

I made arrangements to pick Len up at the hotel that evening in my little brown Toyota. He had been driving all day, I reasoned, and would be delighted to be chauffeured to dinner. Or would he be turned off at the possibility that I was a "take-charge" woman?

I was acutely aware of his eyes on me as I threaded my car through the winding curves leading to the Trapp Family Lodge atop a majestic mountain overlooking the town of Stowe. Parking the Toyota, I glanced at my watch: thirty minutes till our dinner reservation. Another of my compulsions was always to be early.

Len suggested good-naturedly that we walk around the grounds while waiting. The evening sun was setting, brushing the mountains before us with rainbow hues of purple and mauve. I thought to myself, *God is really showing off His creation! He must have a special plan for us this evening.*

We stopped briefly at the small family cemetery where Baron von Trapp and other family members were buried beneath scrolled wrought iron crosses. Pansies, larkspurs and snapdragons bordered each small plot. As we turned to walk across the lawn to the main building, Len reached for my hand, his grasp warm and firm.

During dinner he drew out the story of my life. At first I held back the defeats and failures, wanting him to see only the good. Then something inside said, *Be honest*. I had come so to hate my past deception that it was a great relief simply to tell the truth. Len's warm response further reassured me.

"Would you like to have dessert at my house?" I asked him impulsively.

Arriving at my small yellow house in Montpelier, the first thing Len

saw was a huge brown teddy bear sitting in the front hall, this one wearing a lace dress with a large printed label running diagonally across her chest: *Housemother*.

Len stared at the bear for a moment, then chuckled.

"Housemother is my ferocious protector," I informed him.

Then came a quick tour. As we went from room to room—lace curtains, quilts on the walls, stuffed animals and old dolls everywhere—I was uneasily aware that it looked like the dream house of a ten-year-old.

"What's this?" Len exclaimed as he approached the fireplace. I had covered the low stone hearth with a white linen cloth on which sat twin silver candlesticks, with my Bible in the center. "Looks almost like an altar."

"It is an altar. I spend a lot of time here each day on my knees talking to the Lord. This is also where I have Communion."

"Communion—by yourself?"

"Yes, most of the time. Sometimes with one of the women I'm praying with." I told him how the Lord had been using me more and more to reach out to hurting women.

Taking a deep breath, I blurted, "Would you like to have Communion here with me now?"

Surprised, Len's eyes searched mine. Then he nodded.

I returned from the kitchen with a goblet of grape juice and two round wafers on a small glass plate. We knelt together and Len read from 1 Corinthians 11:23-26: "The Lord Jesus in the night in which He was betrayed took bread; and when He had given thanks, He broke it. . . ." We served each other "the bread of life," then "the cup of salvation."

Afterward Len took my hand and prayed, "Lord, we are Your children, committed to You, eager to have You in charge of this relationship." Something deep and important happened to us as Len said those words.

And so God was there with us from the start. At my invitation Len returned to my house the next morning for breakfast, handsome in a navy cotton shirt and red, white and blue checked slacks.

Noticing a third place setting at the table, he asked: "Are you expecting someone else for breakfast?"

"That's the place I always set for the head of this house," I replied.

When Len looked startled, I explained, "Jesus is my husband and the head of my home."

"That's great, Sandy. I love it." His eyes were misty as he spoke.

We had lunch at Peacham Pond with my friends Margaret and Frank—she of the hotel room refurbishing. After eating I asked Len if he would like to go for a walk in the birch-strewn woods. "Ah—a chance to smell the flowers," he said.

The August sun warmed us as it filtered through the canopy of leaves. Hand in hand we laughed and talked together. How I had longed for such a relationship!

Suddenly Len spied a patch of lady's slippers growing among a lush bed of ferns. He bounded playfully toward the flowers, knelt down and buried his head in the lavender blooms.

"Hey, no smell," he said, disappointed. Then he turned to me with that reflective look I was getting to know. "My mother used to tell me I needed to take time to fill my soul with beauty. She'd be pleased that I'm doing just that today."

His 92-year-old mother, he told me, was comatose in a nursing home in Gaithersburg, Maryland.

Now came the moment I had been waiting for. Pointing to a large birch tree by the side of the path, I exclaimed, "Look, Len, there's something sticking out of that tree."

Len went over to investigate, retrieved a zip-lock baggie tucked beneath a protective layer of silver bark.

"Open it up and see what it is."

Len gave me an inquiring look, undid the small plastic bag and read aloud the note inside: "Welcome to Peacham Pond, Len. Blessed is the man whose trust is in the Lord."

He was clearly dumfounded. "You did this. But how did you know I'd be here today? I didn't know myself until last night."

"I didn't, either. But I hoped—and planned this surprise for you."

"You do indeed major in surprises." Len took both my hands in his, leaned forward and kissed me lightly on the lips.

*   *   *

Len had an appointment the next day in upstate New York, but promised to return to Montpelier Tuesday evening before heading south again.

Late Tuesday afternoon he phoned to say he was back at the Montpelier Tavern Inn—exhausted with a headache. "I'll be as good as new after a nap," he assured me.

Another challenge! I decided to prepare another first-aid kit, but this time deliver it myself—as a nurse.

I pressed a white cotton dress quickly, donned it, then took stock. What to do for a hat? Out of a piece of white construction paper I fashioned a nurse's cap, adding a black stripe and a large red cross in the front.

Needing a nametag such as nurses wear, I cut a three-inch heart from the same construction paper and printed on it *Nancy Nice Nurse*. That should do for a start, I laughed to myself, surveying the white figure staring back at me from the bathroom mirror. I did look like a nurse!

The first-aid kit consisted of band-aids, athlete's foot spray, aspirin and other medications in a small basket. I concealed basket and cap in a shopping bag and slipped a raincoat over my strange white outfit. In the hotel lobby I rang Len's room.

"O.K. if I come up? I've got something to help your headache."

Len opened the door to my knock and stared in disbelief. "Nancy Nice Nurse? I can't believe this!" He laughed until tears ran down his cheeks.

The idea of God as a matchmaker transformed our courtship into high adventure. From the beginning, starting with that Communion service, we prayed together. After get-togethers all the way from Vermont to Florida, we asked this of God: "Lord, if it is Your plan for us to marry, open every door along our way. If it is not Your plan, close the door."

So trust in God and His instructions about our future became the cornerstone of our courtship.

How different this was from the get-my-own-way atmosphere of the courtships prior to my first two marriages!

Early on Len revealed that his first marriage was to a beautiful New

York City model named Eve. After trying for nearly ten years to help Eve overcome her bondage to alcohol, in great agony and with a sense of total failure Len filed for divorce and was given custody of their three small children. Then, feeling helpless and inadequate as a single parent, he turned to God for help in finding a new mate.

God responded in an amazing way. In 1959 He led Len to a woman whom, on his own, Len would never have considered approaching— Catherine Marshall, a bestselling author and Christian celebrity. Len and Catherine had a fulfilling and productive marriage for 23 years.

When Catherine died in 1983, Len was 64. After a year and a half as a widower, he turned once again to God, praying, "Lord, You know how I need a partner! I will accept every invitatio.1, keep on the move so that You can direct my steps to the woman You choose for me."

Only a few weeks later Fred Bauer introduced the two of us.

Early on, I could sense in Len a wariness about my alcoholism— understandable after the agony of his first marriage. During our courtship he kept asking God, "How can Sandy and I be sure that this marriage is Your plan for us?"

His answer came in two words:

Trust Me.

Over and over in the weeks and months that followed: *Trust Me.*

Sometimes there were additional instructions.

Make yours a scriptural romance.

We interpreted this to mean that first we were to get to know each other spiritually, mentally and emotionally, and to get to know each other's families. The sexual relationship would be blessed after marriage.

Learn to have fun together.

For Len this bit of guidance was a surprise. A workaholic type, he admitted he had much to learn in this area.

Both of us were amazed at the joy and deep fulfillment to be found in courtship on God's terms. Those drawn together through physical attraction alone miss the heights and depths a romance can have. For after all, the God who created love knows how to tune two human hearts to thrilling harmony.

When you ask God to be a matchmaker, here are a few guidelines to help bring you into contact with the mate He has for you:

1) Accept that it will happen in His timing, not yours.

2) Go to places where your future mate might be (church, social gatherings, community meetings, sports events, etc.). It's unlikely you'll meet him or her in a bar.

3) Pray before turning down an invitation you ordinarily wouldn't accept. You may need to widen your acquaintances, broaden your interests before God can act.

4) If you meet someone you like but to whom you are not attracted physically, give it time. It is possible to fall in love with inner qualities more than outer.

5) Overeagerness is often a turn-off. When you meet someone you like, ask the Holy Spirit within you to take control. He will, in surprising ways, if you let Him.

6) Trust God as your best possible matchmaker. Trust Him to bring you and your future spouse together. Trust Him to guide you through a time of courtship. Trust Him to tell you both the right time to become engaged, the right date for your marriage. Most important of all, trust Him for the rest of your marriage.

Scripture always says it best: "Trust in the Lord with all your heart, and lean not on your own understanding; in all your ways acknowledge Him, and He shall direct your paths" (Proverbs 3:5-6, NKJV).

—4—

The Perils of a Perfectionist

$\mathscr{R}$ECOVERY $\mathscr{P}$RINCIPLE # 4
Accept Yourself

$\mathscr{I}$ don't know how or when I became a perfectionist. Perhaps it was hereditary; my mother has always been one, especially about cleanliness. Or perhaps perfectionism is just one of many faces of compulsiveness.

In any case, I remember back in junior high deciding I wanted to be a majorette. I practiced for hours with the baton, whacking at my knobby elbows in my spastic attempts to twirl like the big girls. My arms and legs were such a welter of bruises I might have been taken for a victim of child abuse! Never mind. I was dogged in my determination to master the spins and whirls and figure eights I had seen real majorettes execute.

That summer I enrolled in the school playground program. Our instructor, Shirley, was a majorette at Spaulding High School. I had seen her march and thought she was as glamorous as any Hollywood star. I spent hours in front of the mirror in my bedroom trying to do my hair just like Shirley's. I begged Mother for white canvas shoes like hers.

Shirley graduated and I switched my hero worship to Greta, who lived next door. Greta was also a majorette at Spaulding and often practiced on the front lawn. Shy, I watched her at first from behind closed curtains. She was poetry in motion. One day I mustered enough courage to ask Greta if I could twirl my baton along with her. She graciously consented and became a loving mentor and friend, the older sister I never had.

In my freshman year at Spaulding High I was a nervous wreck for days before tryouts to replace four graduating majorettes. I could barely eat. My studies suffered. Everything suffered. I suffered most of all.

Tryout day arrived. My palms sweated as I clutched the baton. The rubber ball and tip almost glowed; I had coated them with white shoe polish and buffed them to a blinding brilliance. My baton, after all, had to be perfect.

Whether it was my gleaming baton or the marathon practice sessions, I was one of the four selected. I floated home shouting, "Mummy, I made it! I made it!"

Near the end of the football season new uniforms were ordered for the majorettes. What an exciting day when they arrived just before the final game. We giggled and preened in our shiny new maroon satin outfits. They featured epaulets with silver fringe on the shoulders, satin bands around the cuffs, modest short circle skirts. And for our heads, tall fur hats with brilliant maroon feather plumes!

The last game of the season was with our arch-rival, Montpelier High School. Emotions were at fever pitch, and we majorettes had a new routine to outdazzle the Montpelier majorettes.

Game day came with not a cloud in the azure Vermont sky. We gathered with the band an hour before game time for the traditional march from our high school to the football field. Our new uniforms shimmered in the early afternoon sun as we marched and pranced past the hundreds lining the parade route. My heart was leaping with excitement despite the blisters my new white boots were raising on my heels. We took our places on the front row of bleachers, and the first half of the game passed in a riot of noise and action.

Half-time! Spaulding was ahead by a touchdown. Everything was going right for us.

As the visiting band, Montpelier performed first, while we appraised their routine confidently. We had to admit it was pretty good. But stand back, Montpelier! Prepare to be dazzled.

Our turn had come. Our drum majorette, Joan Plotner, blew her whistle and raised her baton. We were off strutting down the field. Pa dum ta dum. Pa dum ta da da da da dum ta dum. The staccato of the drums cracked like rifle fire through the autumn afternoon. The band separated in neat rows off to the side of the field. Zero hour.

The seven of us stood at attention in our familiar "V" formation, my position last on the left. The crowd roared its approval as we moved into our half-time routine. Batons spun in perfect precision like silver sparklers on the Fourth of July.

On we pranced and danced and spun and leapt. Now for the *pièce de résistance* of our spectacular new routine: the final high toss into the air. The drums rolled, our batons whirled in seven brilliant pinwheels before us. And now the toss. Up, up, up into the air went seven batons.

Looking skyward I caught a glimpse of six spinning silver sticks rising to dizzying heights, then spiraling earthward. But where was *my* baton? I squinted desperately into the afternoon sun.

Thunk! I felt as though a pile driver had slammed the top of my head. The bright afternoon went black, the roar of the crowd faded. I'd gone blind! Deaf! Maybe I was dead. . . .

Looking down, I saw the trampled grass of the football field. Then I knew. Hurtling back to earth, my baton had landed squarely on the top of my tall fur-plumed hat, driving it down over my eyes and ears.

Pa dum ta dum. Pa dum ta dum. The signal to march off the field came while I was staggering around in a circle trying to dislodge the hat wedged over my eyes. It was like prying a bucket off a basketball.

Finally, after what seemed an eternity, I wrenched it off and retrieved my baton from the ground. Utterly mortified, I dared not look at my fellow majorettes—or anyone else. Perhaps the 50-yard line would unzip and the earth would swallow me up.

Joan Plotner blew her whistle. Pa dum ta dum. Pa dum ta dum. Off the field we marched. The crowd was applauding—and laughing. Laughing at me. The perfectionist. The flawless performer.

It was the end of the world. It was worse. The world would go on, and I would have to go on living in it, revealed in all my weakness and imperfection.

In the second half Spaulding won the game and the town went wild with joy. The whole town, that is, except for one girl to whom nothing mattered—not the victory, not the overall excellent performance of the majorettes, not the graciousness and understanding of the others, nothing except that she had failed to live up to the order she had given herself somewhere along the line: Be perfect or be nothing.

By Monday, however, my despair was beginning to lift. One of the star players who had not noticed me before asked me out on a date. What to wear? My outfit had to be just perfect. . . .

As I have continued to struggle with perfectionism over the years, I recently came across the following quiz.* Test yourself, indicating your own response with *Agree* or *Disagree*:

Agree Disagree

_____ _____ 1. I often put things off because I don't have time to do them perfectly.

_____ _____ 2. I expect the best of myself at all times.

_____ _____ 3. I generally think I could have done it better.

_____ _____ 4. I get upset when things don't go as planned.

_____ _____ 5. Other people can't understand my desire to do things exactly right.

Agree Disagree

_____ _____ 6. I am often disappointed in the quality of other people's work.

_____ _____ 7. I feel my standards should be the highest possible, allowing for a clarity of direction and a standard of performance.

_____ _____ 8. If anything I do is considered average, I'm unhappy.

_____ _____ 9. I think less of myself if I repeat a mistake.

*Dr. David Stoop, *Hope for the Perfectionist* (Nashville: Oliver Nelson Publications, 1987).

I answered *Agree* to every statement, which places me in the category of hard-core perfectionist. I see now that while this particular compulsion helped me to succeed in certain areas (like making the majorette corps, achieving high marks at the Rhode Island School of Design and doing well in the working world), it led to deep frustration in the less quantifiable roles of wife and mother.

The perfectionist trait that really undid me was deciding so often not to do something at all unless I could do it "right." If I couldn't have a super birthday party for my small son or daughter, I wouldn't have one at all. If I couldn't get my closet organized perfectly, I wouldn't try even to keep it neat. After a while a sort of paralysis sets in that makes it difficult to achieve anything at all.

Since our marriage in 1985, Len has been helping me fight the "perfection demon." Shortly after we met, in fact, it reared its head— the afternoon I made the "Nancy Nice Nurse" visit to his hotel room. I was watching him chuckle through the items I had put into the first-aid kit when I realized I had left something out.

"The Pepto-Bismol! I left it sitting on the counter." My voice crackled with annoyance. How could I have goofed so badly?

The look on Len's face stopped me. He was studying me with a mixture of amusement and concern. "Sandy, all this was a great idea! I love it—just what the doctor ordered. Why get upset over one little detail?"

Why indeed?

It is the big question for all of us pursuing the fantasy of perfection. For some, even a 99% represents failure. Many of us will allow ourselves no satisfaction short of total success, total achievement.

As a new bride in 1985, I was eager to become involved in activities that interested Len. I knew his two great recreation loves were tennis and bridge. Bridge gave me gastrointestinal distress. I could never remember all the rules nor what cards had been played.

Tennis was different. I liked the clothes. The ambiance. Tennis was something I could learn to do—not just acceptably, not just well enough to keep Len company, but superbly.

Of course, perfectionism dictated first of all that I look the part. In

April it was not hard to find some wonderful Easter clearance bargains on white shorts and tops to wear to my lessons.

My first session at the Gulfstream Tennis Club with tennis pro Fred Horenberger should have sounded a warning. I arrived fifteen minutes early, my stomach churning with little spasms as I pulled into the club parking lot. The busy courts were teeming with leaping white-clad figures.

As I entered the pro shop, I hoped I looked perfect because I didn't feel perfect. The heels of my new tennis shoes pinched against my new terry cloth tennis socks. It was too hot for panty hose, so I had applied erase makeup on the spider web of varicose veins on my thighs.

The lesson began. Fred, a tall, exuberant encourager, cheered me on

BEFORE

AFTER

in his most helpful tennis-coachy way. But I began to realize that my body was in lousy shape. After a short while I was puffing like an exhausted walrus. Before long my new outfit was a soggy mass of twisted fabrics, my leg makeup running in little rivulets onto my snow-white socks. Hardly the pristine vision that stepped onto the court minutes before!

As my errant tennis balls sailed into the adjoining courts, I was aware of stares of displeasure from fellow players. The inability to control the trajectory of these fuzzy little yellow spheres was especially maddening for a perfectionist.

The answer, obviously, was more lessons. After all, I intended to be ready for Wimbledon by the end of the month. (What would I wear?)

I practiced ferociously. I became obsessed with the game. I strategized shots in my dreams and designed tennis dresses in the margins of books. I bleached and starched and pressed my "whites" incessantly.

But I forgot one thing. I was putting enormous, unrealistic pressure on my fiftyish body.

And, of course, the inevitable happened. On the day Fred and I were going to work on my serve, I tossed the ball up over my head. Up went my right arm to smash the ball across the net. *Ping. Pop.* But it wasn't the ball making those sounds. It was my shoulder.

I groaned in pain and grasped the afflicted joint. My tennis career was over before it started.

Most people get tennis elbow. I got tennis shoulder. The white tennis frocks wound up in giveaway boxes and consignment shops. Had I paced myself, been willing to settle for progress by degrees, the results might have been different. But the driven Sandy, the perfectionistic Sandy had to do it all at once. Compulsively. Perfectly. All or nothing.

Perfectionism, I have seen, was one of the factors leading to my alcoholism. Success had to be absolute. The smallest failure was unmanageable. And since some failure in the scheme of things is inevitable, I fled repeatedly into alcohol oblivion.

Bringing all this out with Len helped me begin to deal with it. Also this statement by addiction writer Anne Wilson Schaef: "The way to be perfect is to be perfectly you."

"That's it!" Len exclaimed when I showed him the Schaef quote. "You need to accept yourself just as you are. God created you with strengths and weaknesses. You're a good communicator. You have artistic flair. Develop them more. You're no good with numbers; you have trouble keeping your checkbook straight. So bridge is not for you. You do have athletic coordination, though. If you'd aimed at being an O.K. tennis player instead of a superstar, we could have had fun with it."

I grimaced, rubbing my aching shoulder. "So what's the answer for perfectionists like me?"

We sat down and worked out these five steps for perfectionists everywhere to follow. (I am working at them, imperfectly!)

1) Admit that perfectionism is a compulsive problem in your work and relationships, that you can never fit the dictionary definition: "Complete in all respects; without defect or omission; flawless."

2) Acknowledge that while some good can come out of perfectionism, if it helps you achieve a degree of excellence, all perfectionism has a root of selfishness and self-centeredness.

3) Realize that on your own, with your own strength and willpower, you cannot free yourself from this problem. Relinquish to God your desire to be perfect and ask Him to free you from the inner focus on self that lies behind it.

4) Accept the fact that some of the endeavors you undertake will not meet your high standards; pledge to complete them anyhow. Finish everything you start.

5) Most important, accept yourself. Only the Creator is perfect. We are born with certain gifts, skills, strengths. The challenge for each of us, then, is to find that God-given gift, develop it and use it for the glory of God.

If we could achieve perfection, we would assume a godlike attitude and defeat would surely follow, then self-dissatisfaction and eventually depression. For in our humanness we can be neither God nor completely perfect, though many try.

As a recovering woman I am learning slowly to accept myself and enjoy doing what I can do well. Not that I won't accept a challenge to learn something new, try something different, even stick my neck out. But I am beginning to understand that it is unnatural for us to live in constant stress and tension. Our bodies soon react negatively, our spirits sag, our minds close up. Why? Because we weren't created to live this way.

Self-acceptance is a victory in its own way. It has an inherent element of relaxed power. There is a rhythm to acceptance that is good for body, mind and spirit. Pressure, tension, stress tend to ebb away from the person who knows who she is, why she is here on earth and what God's plan is for her life.

— 5 —

I Won't Be Home for Dinner

RECOVERY PRINCIPLE # 5
Smell the Flowers

If my hangup was perfectionism, Len's was overabsorption in work—the problem his family recognized when they sent him off to learn to smell the flowers.

This kind of relaxation has been hard for Len.

"You need to be a kid again," I told him one day early in our marriage, "learn how to play. That's another way to smell the flowers."

Len looked surprised. "I can be a fun person."

"But it doesn't come naturally. The fun person in you wants to come out, but you keep pushing him back. At times you're enjoying life, then I lose you. You're gone somewhere."

A week or so later Len and I were finishing the dinner I had prepared for the two of us in our own wing of Evergreen Farm. Four lighted candles provided a cozy setting. But all through the meal Len had complained of a mosquito swarm of projects plaguing him. Nothing new about that. Len's list of things to do always filled an entire page of a legal-sized yellow pad.

Now he turned to me suddenly, a light in his blue eyes. "Sandy, I'm discovering things about my work habits."

51

"You mean your workaholism."

"Yes, I suppose you could call it that. To be honest, I've never really accepted that description of myself. Gave lipservice to it only. I love to work, always thought it was healthy for me."

"So what has changed?"

"The discovery that I've used work to avoid disagreeable situations. It began back in my first marriage when I felt so frustrated about Eve's drinking. Nothing I did or said made any difference. So I plunged myself into my work. It was a way to feel better about myself."

"Your thoughts about it may have changed, but your work patterns haven't," I reminded him.

"Not true. There's a big difference since our marriage. I love doing things with you—everything but shopping. I much prefer being with you than with my papers."

I acknowledged the compliment. "But Len, you really haven't learned to say no to people who want you to speak, or write an article, or be on a board or committee. As a recovering addict, I can still see in you the roots of your addiction."

"Come on, Sandy, work is not in the same addictive league as alcohol."

"I disagree." I pointed out to him how subtle workaholism is, that in some ways overworking is harder to kick than other addictions because it draws applause from the rest of us. Work addicts often have thicker denial systems than other people because overwork is rewarded at every level of society, especially in corporate America.

Work addiction destroys relationships and warps personalities. Amid praise and cheers health problems appear, marriages break, friendships dissolve. No one, least of all the compulsive worker, understands what has gone wrong. As their worlds crumble, work addicts respond by rolling up their sleeves and working all the harder.

In certain ways Len and I have discovered together that the perfectionist and the workaholic are similar:

Perfectionist	*Workaholic*
1) Finds self-esteem in being "complete" in all respects.	1) Finds self-esteem in gaining applause for work done well.
2) Obsession to be perfect is a cover-up for deep insecurity.	2) Obsession for work is a way of escaping problems at home or in the past.
3) Roots of the problem lie in a childhood dysfunctional family.	3) Roots of the problem lie in a childhood dysfunctional family.

At first Len believed his workaholism began as an escape from the pain and frustration of his first marriage, and he refused to accept the fact that he came from a dysfunctional family. "My parents loved each other throughout their marriage of 56 years. There were problems, but what marriage doesn't have problems?"

"But Len, you've told me that your mother was a compulsive eater, more than 75 pounds overweight, and that this led to a lot of emotional family upsets."

"True. But food problems are not in the same league as alcohol, Sandy."

"There you go again. Food disorders can be deadly to one's health, devastating to one's self-worth."

"Mother didn't seem to suffer any lack of confidence. In fact, she was an overachiever. She was president of every woman's club she belonged to, a delegate to church conventions, a top speaker. In 1956 she was honored as New York State Mother of the Year."

"What caused the emotional instability, then?"

Len thought for a few moments. "She was a strange mixture of strong leadership and immaturity . . . very sensitive to criticism. I admired her and loved her, but I resented the way she dominated our household through her emotional outbursts. That's how she got her way."

"What did your father do when your mother got upset?"

"He went outside and smoked a cigar."

"What did you do?"

"I took off—to the playground, to my room, wherever."

"So you had already established a pattern of escape from unpleasant confrontations."

Len nodded slowly. "If the definition of a dysfunctional home is a home disrupted by the emotional upsets of one family member, then I guess ours was dysfunctional."

"Mine certainly was," I said. "And in just this area of workaholism. It's why I'm so aware of the damage it can do."

I can still remember greeting my grandfather late on Friday afternoons when he returned from his week-long shift on the Boston and Maine Railroad. When I saw him appear over the crest of the hill, I would bound out the screen door and run to him. He would drop his metal lunch bucket and scoop me up into his arms with a bear hug.

"How's my honey bird?" he would always say. His engineer's clothes smelled of creosote and tar as I buried my head into his shoulder. Grandpa saw his family only on weekends.

As I look back on all the males in my family, a common trait is evident: They worked hard. And when they weren't working, they talked about all they still had left to do—an endless litany of "shoulds" and "have to's" and calls during the day saying, "I won't be home for dinner."

The women, too, were occupied constantly. In a household devoid of modern conveniences, it was literally true that "a woman's work was never done."

I remember my grandmother ironing with a heavy old cast-iron contraption with removable bases that she kept heating on the back of the kitchen woodstove. When one cooled off, she would snap on a red-hot alternate. Ironing was a major project: sprinkling the rumpled, line-dried cotton clothing with hefty shakes from a water-filled Coke bottle, rolling each garment into little jelly rolls, wrapping them in large terry towels so they wouldn't dry out.

I would watch her for hours, chatting from my child's "junior seat" next to the kitchen table. I felt so important when she let me fill the Coke bottle and sprinkle the clothes!

Gram would stand for hours at the creaking wooden ironing board, looking fragile, her snow-white hair captured beneath a pristine white hair net. Her cotton housedress and apron were always starched, the stays of her corset forming ridges at her waist, her sturdy black work shoes tied with double knots.

On summer days I worried about her, she looked so hot and exhausted; but never a word of self-pity interrupted her ritual. When tiny rivulets of perspiration trickled down her temples, she would dab at them daintily with an ever-present white batiste hankie.

Stoic and uncomplaining, she became for me a model of virtuous womanhood.

"... A WOMAN'S WORK IS NEVER DONE."

Both my parents were raised in small New England communities, Dad in Vermont and Mother in Maine. The work ethic was the way of life in rural New England. My parents had experienced the Depression and were wary. "Work hard. Don't be caught napping. Save for a rainy day."

I never saw my father sit idle. When he wasn't at work selling appliances or automobiles, he was home mowing the lawn, papering, painting, tinkering with broken motors. His life was a litany of movement. Doing. Hurrying.

My mother, too, was constantly busy around the house. Dusting. Polishing. Cleaning. Washing. Ironing. I don't recall her taking time for leisure, to enjoy herself or to have fun. I used to wonder if she knew how!

Looking back at my family in the light of Len's work-oriented philosophy, I saw a sad procession of unhappy, unfulfilled people who felt they had to "earn their salt," perform to be accepted, forsake pleasure and leisure, toil at repetitive tasks to avoid having to deal with feelings.

The result: a dysfunctional family. Any home where feelings are not expressed—just as any home where feelings are used to bully and manipulate—produces emotional cripples.

Like so many others in my family, I was geared to be a workaholic, but as a doctor's wife with three small children I could hardly become a working mother. My husband would have forbidden it. So I became a compulsive volunteer.

Helping community causes is most worthwhile. I wish I could say I did it for the right reason—because of an unselfish, caring heart. Sadly, I see now it was an ego thing. Being on committees made me feel important, valued.

The children had good care at home, I rationalized. Though my heart was pricked with guilt at the bewildered little faces of my children as I whirled in and out of the house, my motor was running out of control. "You've got to produce to be somebody," I told myself. And my new "career" became volunteerism.

At one time I was decorations chairman of the Billings Symphony Ball, spending hundreds of hours making little black-and-white flowers, gluing jillions of sequins and feathers and doo-dads. I was newsletter editor of the Billings Junior League, community service chairman of the Auxiliary to the Montana Medical Society.

Any one of these jobs would have been more than enough. I took them on all at once. If I had not been institutionalized, I'm sure I would be dead today.

As Len and I had done for my perfectionism, we drew up a series of steps for him to follow out of work addiction and into a more balanced life:

> Slow down.
> Learn to say no.
> Rest for an hour each day.

No work on Sunday.
Learn how to play.
Find more time for family.
Take long walks.
Eat fewer fats and sweets.
More discussion of feelings and emotions.
Attend a twelve-step support group.

– 6 –

How Can I Wash Her Feet
If She's Wearing Pantyhose?

$\mathcal{R}$ECOVERY $\mathcal{P}$RINCIPLE # 6
Obey the Inner Voice

$\mathcal{M}$arriage to Len plunged me into a series of encounters that tested my new relationship to the Lord and everything I had learned during five years of sobriety. While Len and I won the acceptance (and eventually the love) of our new family members, a few friends and associates of Len's and Catherine's were less than enthusiastic about my arrival in their midst.

One such friend was a board member, along with Len, of the Breakthrough prayer ministry. As Len's wife I had been voted into board membership soon after our marriage. My first "official" board meeting was in our own home over a three-day period with me as hostess. I was in a panic, in perfectionistic overdrive.

Living room chairs were set up in a circle for nine people. Nervously I fretted over the red-and-green-plaid Christmas decorations still in proliferation. Didn't everyone have their holiday decor intact in February?

It was always hard for me to admit that Christmas was finally, truly over; I decided to leave the ornaments where they were—including the little brown teddy bears I had attached to the crystal chandelier (a prized possession of Len's mother) that now hangs over the dining room table.

Len had regaled me with stories of his mother's Christmas parties in the 1930s when she would go out on Christmas Eve and buy up as many trees as she could find at bargain prices, transforming their Newton, Massachusetts, home into a winter wonderland. I understood this lady and felt somehow that she would approve of my compulsive style.

We had hired extra help to prepare meals for the board meeting, and the kitchen was abuzz with whirring and sizzling sounds. Everything was under control—except the butterflies in my stomach.

I had met the board members at the previous meeting six months before when Len and I were newlyweds. I remembered how nervous I had been when I entered the room and felt their friendly but close scrutiny. One woman who especially concerned me was Virginia Lively, a nationally known speaker and retreat leader. A tall, stately woman with penetrating blue eyes and an almost palpable aura of wisdom and depth, Virginia had been one of Catherine's closest friends.

I had sensed how hard it was for her to see me in Catherine's place. She had loved Catherine very much. In the presence of her still-fresh grief I had felt like an intruder. How could I or anyone else ever measure up to Catherine?

And, of course, I had promptly forgotten every recovery skill I had ever learned. My face had flushed. My hands had turned to ice. Rivulets of perspiration had run down my back and I had been convinced my deodorant was failing me. Before the evening was over, however, I had been voted unanimously onto the board.

Now, six months later, I was to be hostess for this same group.

The first evening was set aside for personal sharing. Again I felt in awe of these people, all with writing, teaching and prayer ministries that have had worldwide impact. I found myself trying hard to accept the fact that I was married to Len and part of this influential group.

The next day, as business matters were taken up, I focused on my duties as hostess, trying to be as inconspicuous as possible during discussions. After all, what could I with my short experience as a Christian contribute to compare with the expertise of these giants of the faith?

Again, I was terribly conscious of Virginia's strong presence and what I felt was her silent disapproval of me.

That night when Len and I went to bed, I silently thanked the Lord for seeing me through the day. A final meeting tomorrow morning, then lunch and it would all be over!

Len's steady breathing next to me indicated he had long since fallen asleep. I was strangely annoyed that he could sleep anywhere, anytime—a skill he said he had learned as an editor working at all hours. Lying there sleepless, I felt like the fabled "Princess and the Pea." Our mattress had never seemed lumpy before; now every crease and indentation irritated.

"Sandra, go to sleep," I kept ordering myself, to no avail. The idea of praying finally occurred to me. "Here you are on a prayer ministry board and praying is the last thing you try," I scolded myself.

"Lord, is there something You are trying to show me? Some reason I'm unable to sleep?"

Silence. And then the tiniest of thoughts in the back of my mind: *I want you to wash Virginia's feet.*

Startled, I was now more awake than ever. Footwashing! I had never done that. Sure, I recalled that Jesus had washed His disciples' feet to demonstrate His humility. And He had asked His disciples to wash one another's feet as a sign of their willingness to be servants, to be reconciled to each other. But no one did that today, did they? At least, no one I knew.

I dismissed it immediately. Wash her feet in the middle of a board meeting? Ridiculous! That couldn't have been God.

And yet . . . the idea refused to go away. At it I hurled first one objection, then another. "There's too much business to accomplish. It would be terribly awkward for everyone involved. And she always wears hose! How can I wash her feet if she's got pantyhose on?"

I'm asking you to wash her feet.

I awakened the next morning to the sounds of rustling pages. Len was already propped up in bed thumbing through the pages of *My Utmost for His Highest*, the classic by Oswald Chambers with which we began our morning devotions.

"Len, I had the most peculiar thought last night just before I finally dropped off to sleep," I told him. "It seemed as though the Lord was telling me—of all things—to wash Virginia's feet this morning at the meeting. Pretty ridiculous, don't you think?"

"Not at all," Len replied thoughtfully. "Let's pray about it."

I sighed. Deep down I knew a footwashing couldn't be my own idea. Where could it have come from but God?

Meanwhile, Len had found the reading for that day, February 19, in the Chambers book. He scanned it, then handed it to me without a word.

> Read John 13. We see there the incarnate God doing the most desperate piece of drudgery, washing fishermen's feet, and He says . . . "If I then, your Lord and Master, have washed your feet, ye also ought to wash one another's feet."

I could not believe the words leaping at me off the page! Of all the days in the year for Oswald Chambers to write about footwashing!

Then a pang of sheer terror gripped me. "Does this mean I really have to do this in the middle of the meeting?"

"There's your answer," said Len. Then he looked at me tenderly. "Sandy, the Lord spoke to you last night, and now this incredible confirmation. He's saying you can trust Him."

The first half of the morning meeting passed in a blur. My mind was not on the agenda or anything anyone was saying. Preoccupied with the task before me, my palms were sweating, breakfast sitting undigested in my stomach.

I stared at Virginia across the room. She looked dauntingly imposing, sitting in the large white easy chair, her crisp, handpainted blouse set off by matching white slacks. The white sweater around her shoulders was trimmed with the same flowers that vined down the front of her blouse. On her feet, white sandals. And, of course, pantyhose.

New objections sprang to mind. Her feet would be terribly uncomfortable if I were to wash them in this air-conditioned room. There is nothing worse than having to sit around in wet hose. She could catch a bad cold.

The 10:30 refreshment break came. Len shot me a "you're-going-to-do-it-aren't-you?" look and I smiled back weakly. He grinned affirmation and love. I knew he was undergirding me with prayer. The word now confronting me was *obedience.*

From the kitchen cupboard I hauled out my largest stainless steel mixing bowl, then filled a large glass pitcher with warm water. Grabbing a hand towel from a kitchen drawer, I headed back to the living room.

The board members were settling into their chairs again, agendas in hand, pens poised to consider the next item of business. My appearance at the edge of the circle bearing footwashing paraphernalia created a shock wave of silence.

Inhaling deeply, I stepped into the circle and positioned myself before Virginia. She looked up at me, startled.

"Virginia, I feel I'm supposed to wash your feet. Last night the Lord showed me that I've had some feelings toward you that I need to confess. The words I heard Him say were *Wash her feet.*"

"If it was His voice," she said quietly, "then you must do it."

I sat down on the floor before Virginia. To me she looked like Queen Victoria in her white outfit, sitting in the white chair. I removed her white sandals gently and placed both of her stocking-clad feet into the steel mixing bowl.

Such a touch of class, I thought to myself. *Couldn't I have at least found our glass punchbowl?*

The warm water from the pitcher poured over her right foot, turning her hose a dark brown.

"I need to ask your forgiveness, Virginia," I said as I washed the foot, "for some negative thoughts about you, thoughts that come from my own insecurity."

I lifted her right foot from the bowl and dried it. Next, the left foot, the same procedure.

Then I reached up and embraced her, tears of relief and freedom stinging my eyes.

As we broke from the embrace, Virginia's blue eyes glowed with love.

Quickly pushing the bowl, pitcher and towel under the coffee table, I settled into my chair, uttering a great sigh of relief. It was over.

But it wasn't.

The mood in the room had changed totally. The board members sat silent, tears in many eyes. Suddenly one of the women walked across the room to one of the men. "For some time I've held a resentment toward you concerning ———. I feel I can't leave this place today without washing your feet and asking your forgiveness."

She washed his feet and he washed hers.

The agenda went out the window. The Holy Spirit blew through that living room like a hurricane. As one after another knelt to wash someone's feet there were healings and forgiveness and new understandings. We laughed and cried and laughed some more.

And even that was not the end.

Pastor Jamie Buckingham went back to his church and had a "Forgiveness Sunday" as members of his congregation washed one another's feet. Jamie reported to us later that nothing had so bonded his congregation in love and reconciliation as this mass footwashing experience.

And to think how hard I had resisted the inner message, which had gone against every instinct of self-preservation and social nicety!

Later Len and I reviewed the whole experience, marveling at the creative ways God uses to reach us with His guidance for our lives. The sad thing is how often we refuse to hear what He is saying to us. Or we hear but do not obey.

Hearing God is basic, vital and yet so difficult for many of us. Perhaps we expect His voice to command our attention. I am discovering that His voice is usually a gentle thought in my mind, a Spirit-to-spirit communique.

I want you to wash Virginia's feet was a quiet message but a firm one. No way could I slough it off as of the enemy or as coming from my own desires.

How is it that Len and I do at times hear God's voice? We have talked a lot about this and concluded that the more we pray, the more we read God's Word, the more we develop our relationship with Him, the more we open ourselves to receive communications from Him. If we stay close, we hear. If we draw apart, His voice fades. For us, it's as simple as that.

Hearing is one thing, of course, obeying quite another.

I am deeply saddened and convicted by the many requests I have received in my spirit and have done nothing about. It is easy to claim poor hearing or confusion ("I don't understand You, Lord") or fatigue or illness or fear or stubbornness as reasons for not doing what the Spirit tells me to do.

God understands our weak, indecisive natures only too well. He knows we want some confirmation that we are hearing Him correctly. It would have been easy for me to have dismissed the inner voice asking me to wash Virginia's feet as too far out. But the confirmation in *My Utmost for His Highest* on that very date could not be explained away. I would either obey or lose a blessing for many people.

I wonder how many such blessings I have lost in the past by my disobedience?

Going further, I am discovering through this episode that God has a specific solution for every one of my relationship problems, if I but ask Him.

This was a new thought. How would it work with my ex-husband

Werner, for example? So far none of my efforts had lessened the hostility he had for me even slightly.

The key here, I am learning, is that my efforts, coming out of my own humanness, have little power or impact in easing strained, broken or severely ruptured relationships. But God's ways will work.

Wash Virginia's feet. I would never have thought of that in a million years!

So I need to keep asking, then be ready to obey when God gives me His solution.

— 7 —

"I Never Was Pretty, But I Had Good Teeth"

$\mathscr{R}$ECOVERY $\mathscr{P}$RINCIPLE # 7
Give Yourself Away

$\mathscr{A}$s I have moved along on the healing road, I have been surprised by the number of long-forgotten childhood memories that have reappeared. At first I didn't consider them especially significant. Then, as truth emerged through each one, I began to see a pattern of teachings that God was applying quietly to my life.

Like the apple episode when I was a pupil at Miss Hill's kindergarten.

That February morning began as every other winter morning. Mother had selected my clothes for the day and was warming them over the furnace radiator on a wooden rack. Mother believed it was unhealthy to wear cold clothes.

First I had to struggle into the inevitable garter belt with those ghastly hot buckles. On with the awful brown cotton stockings that bunched around the ankles. Into the sensible brown oxfords tied with double knots. The layers accumulated until buttoned, wrapped and swathed I waddled into the frigid Vermont morning like a little woolly Martian bound for Miss Hill's house a quarter-mile away.

Tucked into the pocket of my corduroy pinafore this particular day was a juicy red apple. At naptime when I thought no one was noticing, out came the apple from its hiding place.

Crickle . . . crunch. That first bite echoed through the quiet room like a rifle shot. Miss Hill bounded toward my rest pad and quickly had my apple in her hand. Up went the window shades.

"Roll up your nap rugs, children," she said. "Sandra is going to share her apple with *all* of us, aren't you, Sandra?"

My eight peers shuffled into a lopsided circle as Miss Hill dissected the apple with the skill of a brain surgeon into nine exactly even sections.

"What would have happened if Jesus had chosen to eat the loaves and fishes *all by Himself* instead of sharing them with the hungry multitudes?" she asked. "When we give something we want to others, we become like Jesus."

This unforgettable episode, deep in my subconscious for years, emerged during my recovery process, reminding me again to give of myself. I wasn't basically a selfish person; in fact, my compulsive nature often made me outgoing and giving.

Yet an addiction has a way of eating away good qualities like generosity, faithfulness, honesty. Soon self-centeredness takes over, dominates, destroys one's character.

How fascinating that a bit of wisdom learned in kindergarten would resurface at an unlikely place, the Montana State Hospital, on that sultry night when I got out of bed and comforted the distraught Karen! I had put self-pity aside for a moment as I gave myself to another. And at the exact moment I reached out to Karen, the healing process inside me had begun!

The give-yourself-away principle comes through often in the Bible. "Whatever measure you deal out to others, it will be dealt to you in return" (Luke 6:38). "He who has lost his life for My sake shall find it" (Matthew 10:39).

The principle is implicit in many treatment programs. Andrea, a recovering alcoholic at the halfway house, confessed to numerous suicide attempts. During group therapy we discovered Andrea to be a most articulate communicator. After she finished the course, she was invited back often to share her experiences with other groups. What a lift for Andrea! Seeing herself as a helper and giving of herself increased her self-confidence greatly and hastened her recovery.

Dr. Karl Menninger, the famous Kansas psychiatrist, was asked once what he would do if he felt a nervous breakdown coming on. If the questioner anticipated the doctor's saying, "I would see a psychiatrist," he must have been surprised to hear Dr. Menninger reply, "If you feel a nervous breakdown coming on, lock up your house, go across the railroad tracks, find someone in need and do something for him."

I was struggling with self-pity on Mother's Day in 1986 when I came out of a florist shop. In my hands were two plastic corsage boxes, not just the one I had intended to get for my husband's mother. Each one held a small yellow cymbidium orchid with a yellow ribbon and a pearl stickpin.

"You never know who might enjoy the extra flower," I said in answer to Len's quizzical look as I got into the car.

As we drove to the Gaithersburg, Maryland, nursing home where his 93-year-old mother, Lucile LeSourd, lay comatose, my emotions were spinning wildly. I wanted to pin one of those corsages on myself. For I couldn't ever recall receiving a Mother's Day corsage—not from the father of our three children; nor had I ever trained our two sons to send cards or give flowers (though my daughter Lisa regularly sent me beautiful remembrances that warm my heart).

I knew that my three children loved me very much, that they were proud (and bewildered, perhaps) over my recovery. But little cat paws of self-pity were leaving powdery prints on my fragile feelings this special day. The two orchid corsages lay next to me on the navy leather car seat, their delicate petals quivering rhythmically as our car sped down the interstate toward Gaithersburg.

Hmm, I thought to myself. *I'll just pin one of these corsages on and pretend it's from my sons.*

69

Something checked my spirit. *There you go again. Instant gratification, kiddo. There may be someone at the nursing home who needs this corsage today. Wait. Save it for someone else.*

I resisted thoughts like that. I still wanted what I wanted when I wanted it. Had I learned *anything* in recovery? At times like this I wondered.

We arrived at the nursing facility and the elevator door opened onto the fourth floor. As always the smells and sounds, even in this well-kept, beautifully decorated place, jolted us to the reality of human impermanence, made us aware of our own mortality.

To the left of the nurses' station, several Alzheimer's patients sat in their wheelchairs. Some stared off into another time, others flailed gnarled arms at imagined foes.

Len's mother was just as we had left her a few weeks earlier, her shrunken body motionless beneath the maroon coverlet. Her pale face never moved when Len and I leaned down to kiss her. As Len talked to the still form about their early life together, however, two tears slid down her face. Though she could not move a muscle, she had heard him and responded! Feeling I should leave Len alone with his mother, I slipped away into the hall, picking up the extra corsage as I left.

At the nurses' station I asked if there was anyone on the floor who received no visits.

"Go see Mary in 4G," one of the nurses suggested. "She's a love. You wouldn't believe she's 96."

The door to 4G was wide open. The sun streamed in on a scene I found startling. Seated in a green upholstered chair was an enormous woman. On her head was perched a Boston Red Sox cap, beneath which long wisps of white cotton candy hair fell far past her shoulders. Her bed was covered with stuffed animals.

"Mary, my name is Sandy," I said self-consciously. "I've come to pay you a Mother's Day visit."

"That's grand!" she boomed in a basso-profundo voice that shook her body from the top of her cap to the soles of her fuzzy blue slippers. "Sit down, child. I'm delighted you stopped by to see an old reprobate like me."

I pulled a worn red plastic ottoman close to her chair. Mary's moon face and bulbous red nose gave her the appearance of a kindly Mrs. Santa.

"See that table over there?" she asked, pointing beyond the foot of her bed. "That's about all that's left of my earthly treasures."

Wanting to appear interested, I turned and scanned several old photos, a copy of the Serenity Prayer, a battered cocoa brown leather family Bible and a needlepoint picture of a nurse with Mary's name appliqued on it.

"My friends gave me that needlepoint after I retired from 55 years of nursing," she offered with a noble sweep of her powerful hand. "Nursing was my life. What did you say your name was?"

"MOTHER'S DAY MARY"

I murmured my name, but she never stopped talking.

"I wanted to nurse since I was a little girl. We lived on a dairy farm not far from Boston"—here her eyes filled with tears—"and I was always patching up the animals. Some nights I'd stay till dawn with a sick cow. My dad told me somehow they'd find a way to send me to nursing school. How they did I'll never know.

"My two sisters were real pretty. They got married right out of high school. I never was pretty. There weren't many boys interested in a big moose like me. But I had good teeth.

"I never married and had children of my own," she continued. "But I sure mothered lots of young 'uns as a nurse. I have children everywhere. Of all ages. You'd be surprised how many said to me, 'Mary, I wish you were my mother!' I told them God was just using me to be His voice and tears and hugs. Hurting people need to know God loves them, that our Father God has a mother's heart.''

Her watery gaze moved toward the window. She seemed to be tiring and I sensed it was time to wind up my visit.

"Uh, Mary . . . I'd like to leave something with you before we say goodbye. It's a corsage for Mother's Day. Perhaps you'd like me to pin it on for you?''

Her moist blue eyes flooded with tears as she cradled the oblong plastic container in her large hands. The flower looked so fragile, so jewel-like.

"Oh, no," she said. "It's much too lovely to wear. Let me just hold it and look at it. I always wanted a corsage like this. But not being a mother, no one ever gave me one."

In the rays of the fading sun, the dainty orchid seemed lit from within.

"It's so beautiful it makes my heart hurt," she whispered. "How can I ever thank you?''

I hugged her and kissed her damp cheek.

I thought about Mary all the way home—her lifetime of service to others, her self-discipline. I could see her striding tall in her nurse's whites down thousands of miles of hospital corridors, touching her patients' lives with her warmth.

And now she was winding all this up in a 12 x 15-foot room in a nursing home. Yet she still had her strength and her dignity. I felt privileged to know her.

All the rest of that day my spirit felt lighter. Freer. The selfish addict had given instead of taking.

Weeks later the door to Room 4G was only ajar. I pushed it open gently and walked into a darkened room. The gold drapes were closed. Mary was breathing with obvious difficulty, the long, white hair a tangle on her pillow.

"Mary?" I called softly. "It's me, Sandy, your Mother's Day friend.''

Her eyes flickered open for a moment, then closed. Mary was dying of uremic poisoning and only semi-conscious, the nurse explained.

As I reached down to give her a final goodbye kiss, my eyes fell upon the table filled with her treasures. A shaft of light pouring through the crack in the drapes rested on a shining object. An oblong plastic box. Inside a yellow ribbon clung to a withered tendril of a flower.

It was her orchid. On top of her worn brown Bible.

– 8 –

"I'm Ready to Face 'Old Fang'"

RECOVERY PRINCIPLE # 8
Be Vulnerable

"*No* man is an island."

I don't know how many times I have heard this line from John Donne quoted, but it surely does apply to people in recovery from an addiction.

During the past twelve years, support groups have nourished and sustained me. They represent a lifeline for all of us working at fundamental changes in our coping strategies.

Whenever I felt depression coming on, I went to a support group.

When I was under severe tension or pressure, I went to a support group.

When I had a humiliating experience, a wrenching defeat, a painful loss, I went to a support group.

Today if I have had an exhilarating success, feel especially elated or have been on an ego trip, I look for a support group. I have learned that for a recovering person, any kind of high can precede a tumble into the abyss.

Support groups provide emotional and spiritual sustenance to those feeling low. They have a leveling, sobering effect on anyone who thinks he or she has it pretty much all together. And those of us in recovery need often to be checked by fellow travelers.

Because my husband and I move about a great deal, it seems I am always looking in a local paper for the address of such a group.* Here is a typical recent experience.

On this particular Saturday morning my car pulled into the parking lot of a large shopping center. My stomach was queasy, the apprehension I always feel approaching a new group of people in a family support group. *I hate to be late*, I thought, noting it was five minutes before the hour. Climbing out of the car, I rechecked the address clutched in my hand. Most of the stores had *To Rent* signs posted in their windows. So many people hurting economically.

Inside Room 706 men and women were setting up brown metal folding chairs and placing books and pamphlets on a long table by the wall. Feeling self-conscious, I concentrated on the available literature. Somehow I always felt more secure when my hands were full, and soon my hands bulged with brochures and pamphlets. Did I still need to fill that invisible hole of shame and low self-worth inside?

Even after years of working my recovery program, I realized once again how fragile I am, how uncomfortable in new situations.

People were heading for the circle of folding chairs. I selected a seat opposite the woman who seemed to be directing things. (Often when you sit next to the leader, you have to speak first!)

As I sat down, the pamphlets and brochures I was clutching slipped to the floor in a cascade of paper. When I leaned over to retrieve them, the glasses balanced on top of my head fell to the floor, too. I managed a nervous giggle and settled back self-consciously into my chair.

Gladys, the meeting leader, scanned the room like a mother hen counting her chicks. "Let's get started and introduce ourselves," she urged. One by one we gave our first names.

Obviously Gladys was a veteran of support group meetings. I was taken by her Easter-egg-like appearance. Thin legs protruded from a round body clad in a purple and red Hawaiian shirt and shorts com-

* See pp. 197–206 for the various headings under which these are listed.

bination. Her fuzzy salt-and-pepper hair was pulled back over her ears with two sparkly red barrettes; scarlet sandals housed her magenta-painted toes. She ran the meeting like a Marine drill sergeant.

Two chairs over from Gladys was Wanda, a divorced mother of three. She spoke first, running fingers through her long, black hair. "Say a little prayer for me. I'm flying to New York for my daughter's wedding next weekend and *he* will be there."

Several people in the group nodded; *he* was obviously her ex-husband.

But Wanda talked mostly about her mother, a manipulator who had decided her daughter couldn't handle the pressure of this event. Mentally I could envision little girl Wanda under the thumb of a controlling mother who made every decision for her. Now, however, there was something triumphantly defiant in Wanda's pale green eyes.

"I said to her, 'Mother, I can handle it.' I've come a long way in my alcohol program and I have the tools to get through an unpleasant encounter with 'Old Fang' and not fall apart. I do not intend to miss my daughter's wedding just because her father is going to be there. Maybe last year I couldn't have made it, but I can now. I feel good about myself and who I am."

I studied Wanda as she carefully rearranged the front of her over-sized purple satin shirt that covered a ribbed black tank top. She was bra-less. Pretty brave for someone in middle age, I thought. Then I noted quarter-shaped calluses beneath each kneecap. Were they from a charwoman's work or years on her knees in prayer? She punctuated her speech by stabbing her index finger into the air, causing her purple metal earrings to swing about her face like chandeliers in an earthquake. Wanda, I concluded, could take care of herself. Her mother's days of domination were over.

The subject of the meeting was "letting go," a subject wrenchingly difficult for most of us.

Now Gladys told her story, in a way that indicated to me she had recited it countless other times.

"My husband was wounded in World War II and this guy hasn't given me a moment's peace ever since. Nothing is ever good enough or fast enough or hot enough or cold enough. He's negative, negative, negative from the time the sun comes up, and he made my life a living hell till I started to come to 'these rooms' [a term you hear at many meetings].

"I've come to realize I am not responsible for how he thinks or what he says. I have to take care of Numero Uno." Gladys was drumming her chest with her fingers. "You know where I am now? I've let go of him and his power to get to me and keep me crazy."

She signaled the end of her remarks by folding her large arms over her bulging midriff and recrossing her knobby knees.

Kitty spoke up next. "This must be husband and ex-husband day," she joked, glancing apologetically at the five men in the circle. "Please forgive me, fellas, but all the guys out there aren't as nice as you! It's like my ex-husband has checked out on all responsibilities where our three grown children are concerned. He never writes or calls or pays

any attention to them. They try to shrug it off, but I can tell they feel rejected and abandoned.

"This program has taught me that I need to let go of any expectations where he is concerned. For years I tried to make up for his lack of concern, financially and emotionally, and it darn near killed me. I've got to face the fact that I can do nothing about what he does and doesn't do.

"Sarah—she's my sponsor—had a bit of wisdom for me last night when I called her. I was upset that he hadn't remembered our son's twentieth birthday yesterday. No card. No call. She told me to pray that someday he would have the kind of loving relationship that I have with the children. I'd never thought of praying that way for him. In fact, I've been so exasperated with him lately I haven't prayed for him at all.

"But last night after I hung up, I did what she suggested and I felt much better. I felt a release from some of my anger. That's my gem to pass on to you about letting go."

Roger, seated next to Gladys, was clearly unsettled by what Kitty had said, rubbing the toes of his new Reeboks together and jamming his hands into the pockets of his jeans. He had said little about himself, other than that it was his second meeting. Now the muscles of his cheeks bulged as he gritted his teeth, some painful secret gnawing at him. He looked as though he wanted and needed to cry, but was fighting it with everything he had.

A pretty, fiftyish lady seated to my right cleared her throat. "My name is Amy, and I've been listening to all of you talk about letting go. I can let go of some things in my life and I think I have. But there is something that keeps tripping me up. I think I need to let it out.

"My mother always told me that when I was born I so crippled her that for a long time she had to get around in a wheelchair. How's that for a guilt trip? I remember her starting every sentence, whatever the subject, with 'If it hadn't been for Amy. . . .' Can you imagine growing up with that kind of guilt? 'My gosh, I've crippled my mother!'

"I know now that an infant's not to blame, but I still have this old

79

record playing on and on in my brain, *You cripppled your mother. You bad girl. You bad girl!*"

Amy's soft brown eyes were beginning to fill with tears. She pulled at a thread on her peach sweatshirt. "I've always tried to be perfect. The perfect daughter, the overachiever in school, the perfect wife and mother. What a joke. My life feels like it's been one big fat lie. I guess I need to come to more meetings. My mother eventually got better. I'm the one who's crippled."

As in most support groups, the women were more vocal than the men. I hoped Roger would speak up, but he didn't, even when he was asked if he had anything to say. The other men had only brief comments. Most men who come to support groups, I have noticed, have their emotions in check—at least until they have attended a number of meetings.

At the end we all stood in a circle holding hands to say the Lord's Prayer. All ages, sizes, men and women, young and old, blended our voices in the most famous prayer of all time.

I love to hear recovery groups say this prayer. There is something about the brokenness in all of our voices, the weakness reaching out for strength.

As people were hugging and wishing each other well, I noticed Roger bolting out the door. At the end of the Lord's Prayer I had heard Gladys tell him, "Keep coming back. It works if you work it."

Roger's pain must be enormous, I thought. *But he's come to the right place. I hope he comes back.*

Len, typical of males, was reluctant to go to a support group. One day I confronted him about this.

"I'm going to an alcohol support meeting tonight, Len. Why don't you go with me? There's a support group for families held in the same building."

"Why should I?"

"Because it's for people like you. Eve's drinking affected you both."

"That was 30 years ago."

"Well, your current wife is a recovering alcoholic. You may not realize it, Len, but you're a codependent. A family support group will help you see this."

I could see irritation beginning to rise in him.

"Exactly how do you see me as a codependent?" he asked.

I hesitated a moment to think through my answer. "When Eve was in deep trouble, you covered for her, made excuses, helped her avoid facing reality. The goal was peace at any price. In time, without knowing it, you developed a pattern of peacemaking, avoiding confrontation. This is codependency."

He shook his head. "I always thought of a codependent as the wife of a drunk. After a while she depends on her husband's drinking to evoke sympathy for herself. She also becomes the boss in the home. If her husband stops drinking and takes over as head of the household, it's hard for her to accept their changed roles."

"That's one pattern. But codependency is more complex than that. Come to the meeting and find out."

Reluctantly he did.

After the meeting as we drove home together, he didn't say much, but admitted he was glad he had come. There were more women than men attending, he said. A woman had led. She had gone around the circle asking everyone to identify their situations and where they were with them.

"What did you share?" I asked.

"I told about my marriage to Eve."

Len gave no details and I didn't press him.

But after going to several more meetings, he opened up.

"During the meeting the other night I realized not only what a failure my divorce represented, but also that for years I've been trying to block the whole ten-year marriage to Eve from my mind, as though somehow it didn't happen."

He paused, frowning. "We men often do anesthetize our feelings to block out painful experiences. I saw that for the first time."

"Women do that, too," I reminded him.

"I realized something else," he continued. "Though I've been faithful with my alimony support payments and always encouraged the children to maintain a relationship with their mother, I need to do more to try to heal the wounds of Eve's and my broken marriage.''

"Why don't you go and see her?''

Len winced. "She's in a nursing home in Iowa. Confined to a wheelchair. Everyone in our family, many friends, all kinds of alcohol treatment centers, tried to help her. Nothing worked. It's so tragic.''

"When was the last time you saw her?''

"I've talked to her on the phone occasionally, but we haven't met face to face in almost thirty years.'' He paused. "They tell you to let well enough alone in these situations. I wonder.''

Months passed. One night Len's daughter, Linda Lader, called. As she and Len talked, I gathered Linda planned to take her year-and-a-half-old daughter, Whitaker, to visit Eve. Then I heard my husband say, "I think I should go with you.''

Len came back from the telephone looking surprised. "Why did I say that?'' he asked.

"Because something in your spirit said go.''

"Still, it'll be a most difficult weekend.''

But when Len returned from that Iowa weekend, his face glowed. Despite the tragedy of Eve's alcoholism, she had greeted Len with gratitude for his support of her over the years. Len, Linda and Eve had ended the visit by praying together, holding hands and asking forgiveness of one another for all the hurts inflicted over the years.

"A beautiful healing experience!'' Len summed it up. "Why did I wait 30 years to do this?''

Support groups are crucially important to people like me who are attempting to work through past problems. Inner strength comes from hearing others talk about their struggles, which are similar to mine. I can identify immediately with someone grappling with a relationship problem, for example, especially an ex-husband. New thinking comes. I am encouraged to try again in my own life to establish friendlier relations.

Also, the we're-all-in-this-together atmosphere in a support group lessens my loneliness. Feelings long buried because they were so painful bubble up and say, "You have to deal with me!" I don't want to, but I know I have to if I am ever to become whole.

I am always intrigued by the chain-reaction effect a group meeting can have. I returned from one impressed by how a husband was able to forgive his estranged alcoholic wife. He had made an effort to see her and the result was healing. This is why I urged Len spontaneously to do the same, which he did with positive results.

The greatest support group was formed 2,000 years ago. Jesus gathered together twelve hurting, flawed men who would hardly have been called leadership types. They fellowshiped together, had disagreements, shared their hurts and grew stronger together. Their Leader taught them, brought out their gifts. As they were helped, they were able to help others.

And what they learned in a group situation gave strength to eleven of them to go boldly into the world and make an impact that is still being felt today.

-*9*-

Broken Relationships

$\mathcal{R}$*ECOVERY* $\mathcal{P}$*RINCIPLE #* *9*
Be Reconciled

$\mathcal{Y}$ears of alcohol abuse can leave a trail of broken relationships—disappointed employers and co-workers, severed friendships, family ruptures.

Most devastating to me were two broken marriages. One failure is bad enough. Two made me desolate. Depressed and without hope, I tried to end my life. A merciful Lord plucked me out of the miry pit and put me onto the road to recovery, with this word of instruction: *Make amends to those you have hurt.*

Making amends is not something one should do impulsively, however. And I have found there are five categories of such people.*

1) Those to whom we may turn immediately, such as spouses or close family members.
2) Those to whom only partial disclosure can be made, because to do more would cause harm to others. We need always to consider the risks to another's security, privacy and confidentiality.

---

* Drs. Robert Hemfelt and Richard Fowler, *Serenity, A Companion for Twelve-Step Recovery* (Nashville: Thomas Nelson Publishers).

3) Those to whom amends should be deferred until a later date. Perhaps the hurts are so fresh that to reopen them would only trigger rage on their part. Maybe we also need to work through anger and resentments of our own.

4) Those whom we should never contact, because doing so would only open up old relationship doors that need to stay closed. This may be true for a sex addict, for example, who wants to make amends to former partners.

5) Those who, because of death or illness, cannot be contacted. Three techniques can be used when we want to make amends with persons no longer living. One is called the "empty chair technique" in which we imagine the person sitting before us and talk with him or her. A second method is writing letters to the deceased as a form of journaling. Finally, if opportunity presents, we can visit the gravesite to offer our amends through a spoken monologue.

Making amends to my children Brad, Brent and Lisa is something I have been working at for years.

My son Brad is strong and independent. Friends recall an incident at a Little League baseball game when he was nine. An overzealous coach yelled at him for making an error. Seconds later Brad strode off the field and began to remove his uniform methodically, piece by piece, including his baseball shoes. He placed all these items in a neat pile along the foul line and walked out of the ballpark and home in his underwear without a word to anyone, or even a glance at his coach.

Brad never mentioned the incident to me. He never played ball again.

With this same stoicism, he suffered through two family breakups, deciding he had to make it on his own. When I finally became sober, I tried to appease my conscience and undo the harm to my children by giving them material things. They liked that, but it solved nothing and violated the principle of "Don't do for your children what they can do for themselves."

The time came when I had to say a firm *no* to one of Brad's requests.

Soon thereafter I received this letter from him:

Dear ?

I just want to tell you how I feel even though you have never asked me. As a child you never had to wonder where your mother was or if she loved you. All the while you were never being beaten and locked up in closets by babysitters like I was! I had to wonder every day of my life where you were and why you did this to me.

How can *you* expect to be a part of my life now? You weren't there for me then and I don't want you here now. Even if I did, all you would worry about was if I wanted your precious money, instead of your moral support and love.

I don't believe you know what love really is. You have everybody snowed that you had real problems. Well, let me tell you about real problems. Sometimes we have to scrape up pennies just to eat. I helped Brent when he first came to live with me because he couldn't help with the finances. I felt good about helping him. If you are wondering why I felt good helping, it's called that "love" that you know nothing about.

Stay out of my life. Don't write, call or come by. If you want to talk with Brent, make arrangements with him. I never want to hear from or see you again.

Brad

At first I was devastated by the letter. Then I realized it was healthy that Brad had been able to get in touch with the pain and years of rage locked up within him. He was pouring out his feelings to me, gut-level feelings, for the first time in his life. I needed to accept his letter as an opportunity for an honest relationship with my son. I had tap-danced around many issues with him, not wanting to make waves, doing both of us a great disservice.

It was important that Brad know I loved him despite his anger, that our relationship would not dissolve because he had blown up at me. He needed to know I was still there for him, but that I was simply not going to grant his every financial wish.

Our relationship has been much better after this exchange. He learned he could be real with me, vent negative feelings and know that I still loved him.

Brent and Lisa are also learning to express themselves honestly, often bluntly. We are all beginning to communicate on a new level, not speak in the riddles of addictive lingo, skirting issues, telling half-truths or, worse yet, boldface lies.

JUNE 90

BRAD AND BRENT GRADUATE FROM FULL SAIL CENTER FOR THE RECORDING ARTS — WINTER PARK, FL

How best to help my two sons? The answer came through a special course their grandmother and I were able to finance—the Film and Video Productions Program at Full Sail Center for the Recording Arts in Winter Park, Florida. The boys worked hard, spending long hours in all-night labs, filming documentaries, learning every facet of this field.

Lisa flew to Florida from her home in Montana to attend her brothers' graduation. As a special treat we rented men's formal attire: tails, tuxedo shirts, satin bowties and cummerbunds for Brad and Brent to wear with their jeans and tennis shoes. When the four of us celebrated at a pre-graduation dinner, the boys looked handsome in their finery, complete with rose boutonnieres and sunglasses.

Before the diplomas became valid, Brad and Brent were required to complete six weeks of on-the-job internship at a production facility. They were both assigned to station WKCF in Orlando, worked diligently at their assignments, loved the challenge of live programming.

At the termination of the internship, the station manager called Brad and Brent into her office. "I regret to tell you this, but I have only one job. And two brothers. . . ."

Brent came quickly to her rescue: "Give the job to my brother."

Tears stung my eyes when I heard this story from Brad. His younger brother had unselfishly laid down a prize of great worth. Brent would have loved the job. But he deferred to his older brother, wanting to see him blessed with the opportunity. A role reversal here. My sons were now teaching me.

Making amends with my second husband, Randall, was crucial to my recovery. He had exhausted every effort to find help for me and had underwritten the expense of psychiatry and hospitalization. Since there were no children from this marriage, this divorce—painful though it was—was not as destructive as the first one. And my move from Montana to Vermont eased any awkwardness when Randall remarried. An obvious step on my part was to write him a letter expressing my gratitude for his love, support and understanding.

Making amends with Werner, my first husband and the children's father, was much more difficult. Our relationship had been strained and distant since our divorce twenty years before. My attempts to be friendly were usually met with stony resistance.

As in many such situations, the children had become go-betweens, sadly playing roles of wounded messengers with reports from the enemy camp. This always distressed me. I agonized for my children, for the heartbreak and devastation to their lives as they became helpless pawns in our acrimonious marital chess game.

After my marriage to Len, we began a prayer campaign for his ex-wife, Eve, and Werner. Each morning we lifted them to the Lord, asking His healing and blessing on their lives that day. We also prayed that the Lord would open doors of opportunity for reconciliation. This happened, as I have mentioned, with Eve and Len.

One morning while I was shampooing my hair, that inner voice I was learning to obey pounded against my skull like the pulsating jets of water from the shower head.

Call Werner. Ask him to forgive you for giving up on your marriage. His unforgiveness of you is standing in My way of working in his life as I need to.

Was this the Lord? Here was a message that once again I did not want to hear. I did not want to call Werner. He clearly resented any calls made to his home even to talk to our children when they were there. He was so abrupt on the phone that I could hardly complete a sentence.

Len's blue eyes brightened when I reported the shower message. "When are you going to do it?" he asked.

I groaned. I should have known this would be his reaction.

"Soon," I promised.

Though *Do it now!* had become a watchword of my recovery, the procrastinator I thought I had buried resurfaced. *Werner won't be home,* I told myself. *He always goes out for lunch about now. Call him in the morning when he's fresh and rested. And you're fresh and rested.* That was only sensible; I would call later.

Later was a lot later. The longer I put off the call, the more I dreaded the encounter. He would hang up. He would find some way to humiliate me. Days went by.

I felt guilty during our prayer time. I had prayed for a chance to heal the breach with Werner and now I was disobeying the prompting of the Holy Spirit.

Len sensed my struggle. In his loving way, he hadn't bugged me to make the call. But I knew it was on his mind.

Two weeks passed—two long weeks of evasion. The morning finally came when I could put it off no longer.

I sat down on the edge of our bed and stared at the phone. I could hear Len's warm voice dictating letters in the adjacent office. His presence nearby was reassuring.

I dialed Werner's number and waited. The phone rang several times. *He's not home,* I thought with relief. Just as I was about to hang up, he answered.

"Werner, this is Sandra. I need to talk with you about something that I—"

"Yes, I'm quite aware it's you. I'm not sure I want to hear anything you have to say."

"Please don't hang up," I pleaded. "I know how you feel about me and what's happened between us, but I hope you'll let me say what's on my heart."

Silence. At least he hadn't hung up!

"I can't let another day go by, Werner, without asking you to forgive me for giving up on our marriage. And for all the pain and grief I've caused you."

This time the silence lasted for what seemed an eternity. Then, in a thoughtful voice, he responded.

"I can't promise anything, Sandra, but I will try. That's all I can say."

It was more than I had dared hope for. The wellsprings broke open and I began to chatter on about Brad, Brent and Lisa and the plans they were making for their lives.

Then: "Thanks for listening, Werner, and for your openness to what I've needed to say for a long time."

The call was over. I felt jubilant.

Len poked his head around the door. "That wasn't as bad as you thought it would be, was it?"

True. I could have saved myself days of anxiety by being more obedient. My call to Werner had eased the tension between us, but I knew there was much more work to be done. How to relate to a former spouse who lives alone? Werner's two marriages after ours had also ended in divorce. He was understandably bitter about women.

Months passed. Len and I continued our prayers for Werner and Eve. Then Marge Switzer, my closest friend in Billings, and Bob McFarlane decided to be married. I made plans to fly to Montana for the wedding. One morning this prayer came blurting from my lips: "Lord, if I am to contact Werner during my trip to Billings next week, please pave the way and prepare his heart. Make an opportunity available. And close the doors if it's not Your will that I see him."

My trips to Billings were always bittersweet. So many wonderful memories from the twenty years I lived there. But conversely, so many episodes I would rather forget from the worst of my alcoholism.

Now at least I could return with ten years of sobriety behind me. I truly was a new creation; old things had passed away. Or had they?

I especially looked forward to a reunion with Lisa. She had returned to Montana recently to live with her father and attend school. Our relationship had deepened and strengthened, restored by the Lord over the years of my recovery.

The day after I arrived in Billings and the day before the wedding, I felt a nudge to call Werner. I was learning my lesson about heeding these Spirit promptings, so I obeyed. This time Werner's tone was actually friendly.

As we chatted on about Lisa, I felt led to say something I hadn't intended. "Do you know that Len and I pray for you every morning?"

The silence was intense. What he said next I was most unprepared for.

"Do you suppose you could drop by the house sometime while you're here?" He had never before issued such an invitation.

We agreed upon six o'clock that evening, before I attended Marge and Bob's wedding rehearsal.

I shivered in the chilly Montana wind as I rang the doorbell of his ranch-style home on a large corner lot in one of Billings' loveliest neighborhoods. Massive chocolate brown wooden doors stood forbidding before me.

The doors opened and there he stood, taller and thinner than I had remembered, with the ever-present pipe clenched between his teeth. The years had grayed his thick blond hair, but his hazel eyes were warm. It was the first time in many years we had been alone together.

"Lisa just got home from work," he announced. "She's resting down in her room." I sensed his relief that someone else was in the house, and I shared it.

As Werner guided me around his home, I noticed that it lacked the coziness a woman would have given it, but it was comfortable and attractive. A bachelor pad. The tour over, we wound up sitting in the living room in front of a giant TV screen. Werner was obviously proud of his video and sound system.

I settled into a green leather chair across from his tan plush recliner, surrounded by mementos of our life together. On the end table stood the beautiful crystal lamp his mother had given us for a wedding present. How many times had I dusted it?

Over the stone fireplace hung a large, ornately framed painting of majestic Swiss mountains. Werner had bartered for it for days with a local art dealer. How proud he had been the evening he brought it home and hung it in our brick home on Rimrock Road! It was our first painting. And how often I had stared at those magnificent Alps, longing to walk into the painting and wander in that flower-strewn meadow.

I was flooded now by a feeling of sadness for Werner. He had never known happiness in any of his marriages. If only he would trust the Lord to be his matchmaker, as I had.

As he flipped through the TV channels with his remote control, I was struck with a sense of *deja vu*. Just like old times, watching the 6:30 news.

During a commercial break I got up and started to put on my coat. "I have to be at the wedding rehearsal by seven, Werner, but first would you mind if I took a picture of us? I have a camera with an automatic shutter."

"Sure, go ahead." Then he laughed. "We should record this moment for posterity."

The wedding day dawned cold and windy. Lisa was to arrive at the church early so we could sit together. I breathed a sigh of relief as I saw her little black Ford Escort pull into the parking lot. When she got out of the car, though, I moaned under my breath. She wore no coat, only a lightweight sweater, while the October wind whipped her long, auburn hair across her face. The mother in me was horrified to see my daughter shivering in the cold.

"Relax, Sandy," I ordered myself. "She is 28 years old."

How many times I had agonized when Lisa had gone off to high school in freezing temperatures with wet hair and a light sweater slung over her shoulders! Nothing much had changed.

"Sweetheart, where is your coat?"

"Mom, I couldn't find a coat to wear."

What could I say? My instinct was to reiterate all the sermons I had received from my mother and grandmother as I was growing up, but I fought it. Lisa had heard them all anyhow.

The wedding began with an organ interlude. Looking around at the congregation I felt a sense of being home. So many loved ones . . . those who had prayed for me and encouraged me during the dark years. . . .

As the ceremony progressed I glanced at Lisa's lovely profile next to me. She was listening intently. I found myself praying again, "Lord, please gift Lisa with a special Christian man as You have me. Whoever he is, I lift him to You right now."

Lisa was often attracted to "wounded bird" kinds of males —terribly needy, from dysfunctional homes like her own. She was following the pattern of many women drawn to men they hope to "fix," to change into the loving, warm caregivers their parents never were. Nice guys bored her. She felt a need to live on the edge in uncertain, undependable, ultimately destructive relationships. How I longed for that pattern to end for her as it had for me!

After the wedding Lisa came back with me to the friends' home where I was staying. We had barely arrived when the phone rang. It was Werner calling for—me!

"I tracked you down to get your help on something," he began uncertainly. I couldn't imagine what was coming next. "Do you realize Lisa was out today without a coat on? In this freezing weather?"

"Yes, I was distressed about it, too."

"Sandra, when are you leaving town?"

"Tomorrow afternoon at 1:50."

"You and I need to buy our daughter a coat."

I couldn't believe what I was hearing. Werner was inviting me to shop with him for a coat for Lisa!

"I suppose you'll be going to church tomorrow," he continued. "Well, when you get out of church, give me a call and we'll hit the stores. I'll have clipped the sale ads from the Sunday paper. I'm sure we'll find something she'll like."

"I'm sure we will, too," I agreed, still in a mild state of shock.

When I reported the conversation to Lisa, her beautiful hazel eyes stared at me in disbelief. "Dad actually wants to take you and me shopping tomorrow?"

After an early church service, Lisa and I met Werner at his home at 11 A.M. He was ready to go, clippings in hand. Then, just as we were to walk out the door, he stopped abruptly.

"Wait a minute, Sandra. I have something I want to give you."

He disappeared into the living room and returned with a slip of paper, which he handed to me with a flourish. The paper was covered with his familiar handwriting. "It's the secret recipe for the Windmill's barbecue sauce."

Then I remembered. When pregnant with Lisa, I used to crave barbecued spareribs from the Windmill Club, a popular Billings restaurant. I was touched.

"Thank you, Werner. This is really special."

Werner headed out the door for his car, leaving Lisa and me to follow him in hers.

"Mom, you should know that Dad doesn't give that recipe to just anyone," Lisa said, her eyes glowing.

Our first stop was Anthony's Department Store. As Werner steered us to women's coats, he reminded me of many men when they go shopping. Like single-minded hunters, they go out to bag a coat, to "shoot a coat" and do it with as few wasted motions as possible.

He plucked an enormous, plum-colored, quilted garment from a rack. Dutifully Lisa put it on; it was three times her size. In her eyes I saw apprehension. Was Dad going to come up with something really weird?

Since there were no coats her size at Anthony's, it was on to the next stop. I looked at my watch. An hour and fifteen minutes before I had to be at the airport.

Lisa seemed a bit discouraged.

"Don't worry, honey," I chirped. "We'll find you a wonderful coat."

At Rimrock Mall we hit the coat department of every store. By now we were almost running. Lisa tried on coat after coat. Nothing was right.

Werner pressed on. Thirty minutes to go. By now we were at the far end of the mall, Lisa looking doleful.

Then it happened. In the last store on a back rack at fifty percent off hung a beautiful black wool coat with a shawl collar and wide belt. She slipped it over her black print dress. Perfection. Werner was jubilant.

"It's gorgeous, honey," I told her truthfully. "It's you!"

Lisa's eyes danced as she stroked one soft sleeve with her hand. A time for celebration. We asked the saleswoman to take a photo of us linked arm in arm.

"This seems to be a very special occasion," she observed.

"You'll never know how special!" I answered.

The three of us marched down the mall still arm in arm. I looked over at Lisa, her hair flying as we strolled along, a look of sheer joy on her face.

"I just want you both to know," she said, "that I thank you with all of my heart for this beautiful coat. I love it. And I love you."

Lisa would have many coats in her life, but I knew this one would always be special. A coat of love and nurture and togetherness—things she did not always have growing up.

It was a bittersweet moment for me in a completely new way as we strode down the cobblestone mall, laughing and smiling and enjoying the stares of the other shoppers. Let them stare! We were celebrating a reconciliation. Werner's eyes sparkled with new life. He had been a provider. An encourager.

As we said goodbye I planted a sisterly kiss on his rough cheek. Inside were a jumble of feelings: tenderness, compassion, sadness, yet exhilaration, too, at the wonderworking power of prayer.

As Lisa and I drove to the airport, I knew I needed to say something to her that had been on my heart for a long time. But how to say it? How radiantly happy she had been with her mom on one side, her dad on the other. I knew how she felt. It had always made *me* happy to see my divorced parents together.

I found myself patting the arm of her coat. "Lisa, I know how much you love Dad and me. I know how hard you tried as a little girl to fix our marriage, how you agonized and prayed and hoped and finally despaired when we split up.

"Some people shouldn't be married to one another. They just can't make it work." My words were sounding mechanical and tinny, even to me, my effort to excuse myself threadbare. *Why couldn't the marriage have worked?* she would be thinking. *Why did it have to end with so much heartbreak for so many?*

Perhaps I should simply tell her the truth: Her parents were selfish, sinful people who hadn't known God when they broke up.

I thought back to how I had felt as a little girl trying to hold my parents' loveless marriage together. How responsible I had felt for their unhappiness. How hard I had tried to make everything O.K. How desperate and frightened and lonely I had felt. How lost and abandoned.

My voice choked. "Lisa, can you forgive me for giving up on the marriage? For divorcing your father and subjecting you to so much pain?"

Lisa was the nurturing one now. "Of course, Mom. I understand, I really do. I forgive you. It's O.K. It really is."

At the airport gate we clung to each other in a final embrace, tears streaming down our cheeks. Lisa's new black coat had that special store smell as I buried my head in her shoulder.

That night, reporting the Billings visit to Len, I said, "The Lord works in strange ways, doesn't He?"

"Strange indeed," Len agreed. "Who would have thought that reconciliation could be accomplished through a shopping trip and a recipe for barbecue sauce?"

Well, not exactly. I thought back to the day-by-day determined, persistent prayers that Len and I, along with our children, had offered since 1985 for reconciliation in our families. We hadn't known how the Lord was going to do this; that was His business. Our part was to pray and believe. And, of course, to listen to His instructions. And obey them.

Progress had been made. I had a good relationship now with all of my children and with Len's as well. We had taken steps to begin reconciliation and healing work with our living ex-mates—reconciliation that will continue to be needed, I am sure, the rest of our lives.

–10–

The Shopping High

---

*R*ECOVERY *P*RINCIPLE # 10
Identify Your Real Needs

---

*D*uring my battle since 1980 with multiple addictions, I have experienced some definite successes. Alcohol, for one. I know I cannot take even one drink or I am in trouble. As I write this, I haven't had a drink in twelve years.

Smoking, too. Through prayer my craving for tobacco miraculously lifted one day.

Compulsive viewing of television (especially daytime soap operas), excessive exercising, compulsive volunteerism—these, too, I have learned to control.

But not food and shopping.

These two addictions may not seem life-threatening, but because they are ever-present, they are the toughest for me and millions of others to deal with. Unlike the bad habits that can simply be eliminated, we have to eat and we have to purchase a variety of things. Food and shopping are with us always.

Not too long ago I rushed through a crowded mall toward the department store, intent on the shower curtain I needed to buy. With houseguests arriving in the morning, the pressure was on—meals and sleeping arrangements to plan for, all the niggling details a hostess has on her mind.

Once inside the cavernous store, my nose twitched at the whiffs of perfume arising from the cosmetics counter. Like a moth to a flame, I flitted to the Estee Lauder display and sprayed little jets of fragrance on both wrists. The old familiar exhilaration was surging through my veins: *Buy! Buy! Buy!*

As I reached for my purse, a rack of colorful scarves and handbags caught my eye. I walked over for a better look. But wait! There was the best yet—a fifty percent off sale in designer dresses. Fingering through them, I pulled out eight or nine garments for closer perusal.

Then an inner alarm went off in my head.

I didn't need perfume.

I didn't need a handbag.

I didn't need a dress.

I needed a shower curtain.

With a stab of pain I recalled how often this kind of high had led me to spend money I didn't have for things I could do without. Loading my arms with bundles and boxes relieved my sense of low self-worth, made me feel important, cared for. What I didn't realize until I had gone through treatment for my compulsive nature is that shopping can become as addictive as drinking or overeating or smoking or taking drugs.

I comforted myself for years with the fact that I wasn't as bad as some I knew. One friend of mine blew $5,000 at L. L. Bean, the Freeport, Maine, outdoor clothing company, in a one-hour telephone spree. Her husband's annual income was $25,000. Needless to say, her marriage was in grave danger due to her out-of-control spending. She confessed to me that she had felt bored and depressed, that shopping helped her avoid the real problems in her life.

Like my friend, I, too, was trying to purchase self-esteem. Years ago when I lived in Billings, Werner would moan over the credit card receipts I racked up. At one point he revoked my check-writing privileges, until he grew tired of having to handle all the household accounts himself.

In looking back over my shopping excesses, I feel a deep shame for my wanton waste of resources. Anything and everything could trigger a shopping binge. I shopped when I was depressed. I shopped when I was happy. I shopped drunk and I shopped to sober up. "Creative shopping," I used to call it. It was a cry for help, that hole in my soul calling out to be filled.

I see now how cross-addicted I was—from alcohol to food to pills to shopping, whatever would take the pain away.

In *The Compulsive Woman* I described in detail my first shopping orgy when I purchased 22 pairs of shoes and five handbags. I was single then, just starting my first job. I spent an entire month's salary on these items and had to borrow to meet living expenses. But when I was acquiring all those lovely shoes, nothing mattered but the high. The fix.

I shopped frequently when I was angry with Werner. I bought hundreds of dollars' worth of things I really didn't want, as a way to get even when I had been hurt. I felt entitled. I deserved these things, I rationalized—only to be plagued with guilt afterward. Frequently I hid my purchases in the trunk of the car or under the bed.

My drawers bulged with yards and yards of fabric for future sewing projects. Once at a fabric sale (five cents a yard), I came home with 800 yards—enough to have wrapped up my entire neighborhood and tied it with a bow!

That unused fabric proved a source of great creativity for my son Brent, then twelve. One day he decided to redecorate his basement room by hanging yards and yards of cloth from the ceiling like multi-colored hammocks. He draped the walls and windows with huge cascades of fabric reminiscent of a sultan's tent.

Then he appropriated every plant in the house and placed them around the basement artistically on fabric-covered boxes. I had to marvel at his talent. He had transformed his living area into what looked like a Middle East nightclub. We heard the pounding of his hammer at all hours. Brent was trying to bring color and change into the bleak existence my drinking had brought about for him and his brother and sister.

Eventually Brent returned the drooping plants to their original locations. "Guess that wasn't such a swift idea, was it, Mom? I forgot plants need light."

I wanted to hug him, to tell him children could be deprived of essentials for their growth, too, and that I was going to do better as a mother. But I didn't. I felt too guilty. (My response to the guilt, of course, was to go out and buy more fabric.)

Months ago I came across a book that has helped me, *Women Who Shop Too Much* by Carolyn Wesson. I began by taking the self-evaluation test that follows:

Are You a Shopaholic or an Addicted Shopper?
(answer yes or no)

1) Has shopping become the most frequent way you cope with upsetting feelings?
2) Do you feel uneasy without your credit cards?
3) Do you use shopping as a way of making contact with other adults?
4) Are you and the people close to you—husbands, lovers, children, parents—arguing or having long discussions about your shopping?
5) Do you usually hide what you buy or lie about the cost?
6) Do you find that you are not using many of the things you buy?

7) Are you paying only the minimum due on your charge accounts because you are short of money, or because you want to have more money available for shopping?

8) Do you buy items that don't fit your lifestyle—for instance, evening gowns or fancy clothes—even though you rarely have an opportunity to wear them?

9) Are you worried about your shopping?

10) When you shop, do you get a rush or a high, but at the same time feel uneasy?

11) Do you spend six hours or more a week shopping?

12) Do you feel guilty, embarrassed or anxious after you shop?

13) Do you spend more than an hour a week fantasizing about what you're going to buy?

14) Are you preoccupied with thoughts and worries about money, but continue to spend anyway?

If you answered yes to three or more of the following questions—numbers 1, 4, 5, 6, 7, 10, 11, 12, 13 or 14—you are probably an addicted shopper. If that is the case, don't panic. By summoning up the courage to take the test and acknowledge your behavior, you have taken the first step away from addiction.

Yes answers to questions 2, 3 and 8 and any one of the others indicate you may be a shopaholic. That means you use shopping occasionally to fill psychological needs in your life.

Reviewing my own shopping profile—yes to almost every question—showed me that:

I still use shopping to fill psychological needs in my life. I am still too much in the fast lane, still prone to needing quick fixes. I shop to nurture myself.

When I splurge and shop, it often originates from my sense of deprivation as a young woman. I had few clothes in high school as my parents struggled to provide necessities. Morning after morning as I stared at the same few garments, I vowed that someday, when I had enough money, I would have lots of clothes. I fulfilled that vow and then some.

I shopped to look well-dressed and put together on the outside so that no one would know what a mess I was inside.

I labored under the false impression that if I had a closet full of matching cashmere sweater sets and plaid pleated Pendleton skirts—the status symbol of the '50s—I would be happy. I have learned that a closet full of beautiful clothes does not bring happiness, only an insatiable craving for more.

The good news is that since taking the test, whenever I find myself relapsing into the old, destructive behavior, I have been programming myself to go through a change of thinking. I call it the Jesus Factor. (Since my conversion in the Billings Methodist Church in 1980, Jesus has been the biggest factor in my healing.)

The Bible describes "taking every thought captive to the obedience of Christ" (2 Corinthians 10:5). The moment a tempting thought enters my mind, as happened when I went shopping for the shower curtain, I measure it against the teachings of Jesus and the life He lived here on earth. If the temptation counters what I know Jesus would want for me, I reject it.

How does it work? In connection with my shopping addiction, I am learning to invite Him right into the mall or dress shop along with me.

I can only describe it this way. On my shower curtain expedition, my mind seemed like an internal television screen of whirling images, urging me to scoop up armfuls of goods. One of these, two of those—it was like temporary insanity. Unable to shut it off myself, I breathed a quick "Help me, Jesus! Please take control of my thoughts."

The moment I spoke His name, it was as though He stepped from the right side of my mind's screen and walked slowly across it, drawing behind Him a sliding glass door. As the door closed, those tempting clamorous images grew hazy and were soon obscured altogether. A radiant Jesus then turned to me with outstretched arms.

"Let Me fill those empty places inside you that you are striving to fill with things," He told me. "Let My love and grace assure you that you are special to Me. You are infinitely valuable just as you are; nothing you can buy or possess can add to your worth. Rest in Me and be satisfied."

The Jesus Factor has been with me now since 1980, but only recently have I been able to apply it to shopping. Yet I have learned that every slip in any area of my life starts with a tempting thought. That is why I take every such thought instantly to Christ.

Another little victory with compulsive shopping came when my friend Maria Santa Maria and I went to lunch in nearby Middleburg, Virginia. Middleburg is a quaint town filled with historic inns and lovely shops. A great place to take visiting friends!

Before lunch Maria and I wandered into one of the specialty dress shops, The Finicky Filly. A pert young salesgirl announced that everything in the store was thirty percent off, some items more than that. I could feel the old familiar feeling of exhilaration, the start of a high bubbling up.

As Maria and I headed for the jewelry counter, I did take captive every tempting thought. Strands of colored beads and pearls hung tantalizingly from brass racks. My mind went blank. I couldn't remember anything in my closet that would work with any of the beads.

Silver jewelry is my passion. There was lots of it.

But: "I really don't need anything here," I heard myself saying as I fingered a heavy link bracelet lovingly. I could hardly believe those words were escaping from my lips!

My resolve with the dresses was not so firm. Len and I had an upcoming convention that called for a special dress. It seemed I had found it.

It was a beautiful white cotton ankle-length summer frock trimmed with Battenburg lace. I had always wanted a white Battenburg dress, admiring them in the glossy catalogs that flowed into my mailbox almost daily. It was one of my fantasies, sipping lemonade at a garden party in a white lace dress.

The dress fit as though it had been made for me. The deep lace collar framed my face becomingly, and the ruffled hemline was especially feminine. Maria and the salesgirl oohed and aahed. It was perfect. I had to have it.

But deep inside a voice said quietly, *You really don't need this dress. You have other lovely dresses that would work. Think about it for now. Don't be impulsive.*

I didn't like to hear that little voice at times like this. Sometimes I ignored it and plunged on with the purchase, only to regret it later. Still, I knew that the dress, despite the thirty percent discount, was expensive.

"Please hold the dress," I heard myself say to the salesgirl, "while I have lunch and think about it."

What I didn't tell her was that I planned to pray about the purchase, too. Was it something I really needed or was it something I merely wanted?

Maria and I talked about the dress at lunch. It was wonderful to enjoy "owning" it for a while. I pictured myself at the convention banquet, the focus of all attention in white lace. But the inner voice was persistent. I didn't *need* the dress. I had other things to wear.

After lunch I headed for the phone and dialed The Finicky Filly.

"Thank you for holding the dress," I said, "but I won't be purchasing it."

An indescribably warm feeling flooded over me as I wheeled my car out of the restaurant parking lot. I had to smile. The Jesus Factor had come through once more.

He is my comforter, my healer, my helper, my strengthener, my special Friend. A Friend whose love is so all-fulfilling it sets me free of the never-ending pursuit for substitute satisfaction.

My suggestions for the shopaholic:

1) *Do a clothing inventory.* Use a small three-ring notebook so you can add or subtract pages and carry it in your purse. Put clothing into categories: dresses, blouses, skirts, accessories, evening, etc. Attach small swatches of fabric for outfits that need accessories or shoes. This is helpful when shopping for specifics. Make a list of accessories needed. And shop only for those things.

   Sounds tough, but I did it after months of procrastinating. I found my clothing 'way out of balance, but for the first time I knew my wardrobe and was doing something to put it in order.

2) *Be selective in using catalogs*, seeking only items you need. Television star Candice Bergen admits she buys "tons of stuff for the house" from catalogs. "I have a sort of catalog disorder," she confessed in the October 1991 issue of *McCall's*. "My eyes glaze over. I get compulsive. At work they confiscate my catalogs so I'll learn my lines."

3) *Pay with cash*. It is amazing, the impact of counting out cold, hard money as opposed to paying by credit card or even writing a check. Sometimes I have taken only one check, which eliminates impulsive (and usually unwise) purchases. Also tough but effective: Take the scissors to your credit cards. Ouch!

– 11 –

When Bed Was My Hiding Place

RECOVERY PRINCIPLE # 11
Expect the Best

The voice on the other end of the phone sounded unmistakably British.

"Sandra, this is Jane Bolt from British Central TV in Birmingham, England. We'd very much like to do a story on compulsive behavior for our Central Weekend program."

The format, she explained, was something like the Phil Donahue Show. "Would you be available to fly over for our March 6 broadcast? We will pay all your travel expenses. . . ."

The heady intoxication of a summons from overseas drove every other consideration from my mind. Normally I discuss speaking requests with Len, then we pray about them. But this opportunity was too enticing.

"Yes, of course!" I gushed into the phone. "I'd be delighted."

"Splendid. I'll ring you up in a few days with final details." *Click.*

My ears rang with static from the call . . . or was it the static of excitement?

To my relief, Len was taken aback only momentarily by my unconsidered response. As we (belatedly) prayed about it, he had this intriguing comment: "Go with the expectation that God will use you in a surprising way."

At four in the morning of the day I was to fly to London, I awakened with a throbbing head, raspy throat and fever. Disaster! How could I travel 4,000 miles feeling like this?

Seven A.M. My attempts to medicate my malady had brought no improvement.

"What can I do?" I wailed to Len. "I don't feel good enough to walk across this room, let alone fly for nine hours over the Atlantic Ocean and then go on national television!"

He suggested I call Jane Bolt to see if I could do it another time.

"Oh, no!" Jane gasped into the phone. "My dear, if you don't come we'll have forty-five minutes of dead air! Can't you bundle yourself up with your aspirin bottle and hop on over?"

"I'll give it my best shot," I croaked into the receiver.

A decade earlier I would have used this fever to collapse into bed— for days, weeks. The slightest ache or pain gave me an excuse to retreat from responsibility, to seek attention, to take the focus off my drinking. Soon I would be in bed, phone off the hook, pillow plumped under my head.

Hypochondriac? In some ways, yes. But the teaching I received at the treatment center, halfway house and in support groups convinced me that fleeing to bed is not a solution to emotional problems. Today I am much more in touch with my feelings, have much to live for and hate to go to bed.

It was Joy Dawson, Christian prayer leader and teacher extraordinaire, who challenged both Len and me that an illness need not keep us from doing the Lord's work. Joy has a dynamo inside her that gives her seemingly inexhaustible energy. She would brush that aside, saying, "The Holy Spirit will give that to you, too."

I am convinced that only hospitalization, or perhaps a raging fever, would keep Joy from a Christian commitment. She would get up from a sickbed, trusting God to give her what she needs. Once she awoke with severe laryngitis the day she was to give a major speech. Though her voice was but a croak, she dressed, arrived at the event and stood before her audience *expecting the best*, in faith. The first few words came out in a whisper; then, slowly, her voice returned to full strength.

Was this my opportunity to test Joy's premise?

We started out by seeking extra prayer support. Len phoned a number of prayer warriors while I dragged myself through the motions of packing—sniffling and hacking all the way. The fever refused to abate despite megadoses of aspirin. My eyes were swollen almost shut.

I sensed that Len was about to assume husbandly authority and call the whole venture off when at two P.M. there was a near-miraculous change. My physical symptoms all but disappeared as renewed energy poured through me.

"I feel better!" I marveled to Len. "The prayers are being answered."

I couldn't wait to find out how God would use this overseas adventure!

The flight over was a blur of faces, interminable offerings of food and an almost sleepless night. Going through the customs line at Heathrow took an eternity. The sun was up when I met the limousine driver in the arrivals area arranged for by the television station. Two hours later we arrived at my hotel in Birmingham.

I had barely thrown my garment bag onto the bed when the phone rang. Jane Bolt and Sue Gay, the Central Weekend hostesses, would be right over.

I opened the door to two bright, shining faces.

"You look wonderful!" they encouraged me. "No one would ever dream you were so ill a few hours ago!"

The live one-hour show went on the air at nine P.M. At seven I arrived at the station armed with three copies of my book and wondering who the Lord would nudge me to give them to. That was part of the adventure of any trip.

Book one went to the makeup girl. A frail wisp of a brunette named Bridgette with inch-long scarlet fingernails, she flicked at tears as she poured out her heart to me regarding her marriage problems.

Jane Bolt appeared in a flurry of gold chiffon and led me down a maze of halls into the brightly lit studio.

"Marshall, dahling," she crooned to an orange-haired pot roast of a man wrestling with a headset, "this is Sandra LeSourd, the compulsive woman."

Marshall shot out a hand studded with diamond rings and squeezed my clammy one. "I loved your story about buying all those shoes. We'll want to do a shot of you surrounded by a mound of shoes."

Had I flown 4,000 miles for this? The most bizarre TV experience of my life was underway.

All of us participating in the show were herded into a corner of the studio where the air conditioner blew out great blasts of frigid air to counter the blazing lights overhead.

My teeth started to chatter uncontrollably. *Please, Lord, help me get through this program.*

Marshall was bouncing all over the set, dodging cables, barking signals into his headset, waving his clipboard in the air with diamonds flashing. His main concern seemed to be an enormous glass bowl heaped with hard-boiled eggs. "Did you boil them long enough? Do we have eighteen? Where is the stopwatch?"

Gradually I became aware that the main attraction of the program was a certain man named Peter, holder of more Guinness World Records involving eating and drinking than any human being alive. Tonight before our very eyes—and those of the millions tuned in— Peter was going to try to break his own previous egg-swallowing record.

For the compulsivity segment of the program, I discovered, some twenty people had been assembled. How could there possibly have been 45 minutes of dead air without me?

The lights dimmed. Show time!

The first segment featured two gentlemen from Parliament who engaged in a furious exchange over a killing in a neighboring village. At issue: What punishment for the attacker? Anger erupted. Men and women in the studio audience jumped to their feet shouting, demanding justice.

I was beckoned to a side set where a beaming Sue Gay awaited me.

"You're going to love this show. We've rounded up some really fascinating guests for your segment."

Right above my head the air conditioner belched icy gusts at me. My skin was turning blue, my nose running furiously. I wadded lumps of tissue up each nostril, then tried to talk. "Huddo, my nabe is Sander-ah. . . ."

"Welcome to this evening's special feature on compulsive behavior," Sue purred into the camera. "Tonight our special guest is Sandra Simpson LeSourd, author of *The Compulsive Woman*, who has flown all the way from Florida to be with us tonight. And now for a look at sexual compulsions, here's a film clip from the popular movie *Fatal Attraction*."

The grisliest scene of the movie rolled for our edification. Knives flashed. Blood gushed.

Next, a full-screen shot of a grizzled sailor resembling Jack the Ripper. A trembling young woman related how this sexaholic was terrifying her with phone calls and beating on her door in the middle of the night.

Backstage, Marshall was losing his mind. Where was the man with the stopwatch? Did they have enough eggs? He gave the signal and a velvet-draped table was wheeled to center stage.

Now from behind maroon curtains burst Peter, his pockmarked face glistening with perspiration, his bulbous stomach protruding over his belt buckle. Settling his enormous frame behind the table, he reminded me of a Japanese sumo wrestler preparing to demolish a hated enemy. For Peter the enemy was a massive bowl of tubercular-looking gray eggs wilting under the intense TV lights. At Peter's left a nervous stagehand stood poised to activate the stopwatch that would verify for the world a new egg-swallowing record.

A drum roll underscored the taut scene.

"Now!" Marshall shouted. *Click* went the stopwatch. Peter dove into the bowl of eggs. One down. Two. With each gulp an egg disappeared into the huge, quivering, tattooed body. Peter's face was turning purple. Bits of yellow yolk tumbled onto his *Guinness World*

Recordholder T-shirt. The bowl was emptying fast. Marshall was breathless.

Victory! Peter had broken his own world record, eating eighteen eggs in nineteen seconds. Marshall's face burst into a jubilant grin.

When the host asked Peter why he continued to break his own records, he replied—stifling a mighty burp—"So that my children will have something to be proud of their father for."

There followed multiple short interviews: a workaholic, a woman who went compulsively from relationship to relationship, a psychiatrist with bushy hair and a yin-yang earring who specialized in addiction problems.

I was struck especially by a fragile girl named Debra who suffered from obsessive-compulsive disorder, dressing and undressing fifteen times in the same clothes before she could go out the door to work. Needless to say, she was usually late and had been dismissed from job after job. My heart ached for her.

Last to be interviewed was a striking brunette named Carol. Her outpourings of frustration and pain revealed an articulate and bright woman.

"I can't seem to win my battle with the biscuit barrel," she moaned. "Why can't I stop my incessant binging?"

Now it was my turn.

"Sandra, do you have any advice for these people?"

My nose was running into my mouth in twin rivers. *How chic*, I thought. Freezing in my black chiffon evening dress, I was sure the air conditioner had frozen my mind as well.

"Most of us come from dysfunctional homes," I began. "We get trapped in our compulsive behavior." I launched into my own story. But already time was running out.

"Remember this," I concluded. "You can be freed from your addiction if you seek help. Go to a support group. Work some kind of program. There are no hopeless cases."

Sue Gay squeezed my hand enthusiastically. "Marvelous, simply marvelous. One of the best programs we've ever done."

I sneezed.

She led me back through the corridors to a room where a spectacular buffet had been set up for the post-show celebration: carved ice sculptures spewing champagne, fabulous bowls of peeled shrimp, trays and trays of hors d'oeuvres.

In my hands were the remaining two books I had brought to England. To whom should they go?

The woman with relationship problems spotted me and rushed to my side. "Oh, is that your book? I really need to read it." I signed it for her and moved on.

Carol, who couldn't win the battle with the biscuit barrel, lit up as I approached her.

"I can't tell you how much it has helped me just being here tonight," she said, her warm, brown eyes crinkling good-naturedly. "Just having the courage to admit I can't stop eating."

"Good for you, Carol," I agreed. "The first step is recognizing that you have a problem."

A man at her side cleared his throat. "I'm David, Carol's husband, and I want to thank you for coming. I'm willing to do anything it takes to help my wife. Do you have any suggestions?"

Briefly I told them about my own food problems and tried to encourage her to seek help, not knowing what support groups were available in England. We exchanged addresses.

Then, just before we parted, she shook my hand vigorously. "I don't believe in God. But I believe there is some reason I've met you. May we keep in touch?" Her eyes were pleading.

"Write me after you've read the book, Carol," I suggested.

As I flew home, I wondered again why I had made the trip. There had been enough of a physical healing to enable me to appear on the show. Yet my time on it was brief, and there had been no opportunity to honor God. *Lord, was this whole thing just my vanity at work?*

By the time the plane landed in Miami, the flu symptoms had returned with a vengeance. It was a week before I was functional again.

Two weeks after that, a letter from Carol appeared in my mailbox. She had made an important discovery—that anger was the dynamic of her overeating. But what thrilled me most from this nonbeliever was her last sentence.

"I don't know what it is that makes you different, but I want what you have."

My response to her was a package containing *Beyond Our Selves* by Catherine Marshall and *The Angry Book* by Dr. Theodore Rubin.

I heard nothing for months. Then one afternoon in September, five months later, the phone rang. It was Carol, calling from England.

"Sandra, I had to ring you up and tell you in person the incredible events of my life since I last wrote you. I have joined a church in Reddich and tomorrow evening I'm going to be baptized. I have never been so happy in all my life!"

David's eager voice came on. "Thank you, thank you, Sandra, for all you've done for my wife. She's a different woman."

"Don't thank me, David. Jesus is the one who deserves all the credit."

I hung up in a state of shock. Carol had gone from agnostic to baptized Christian in little more than six months. Wow!

My friendship with Carol has blossomed via the mail. Fourteen months after my Central Weekend TV experience, Carol became a member of the counseling corps for Billy Graham's England crusade. Then came a report that Carol's son was freed from anger and soft drugs, had asked to be baptized and was considering Bible college.

"To see him able to laugh, to hear him pray out loud and praise God is beyond belief," Carol wrote.

She now does visitation work for her church, helps organize local Christian rallies and, along with her husband and son, is setting up a youth club. (Carol's son plans to attend Bible college.)

I guess the words that touched me most came in her most recent letter: "That night on the TV program here in England, you shone like an angel, Sandy. In fact, you were my saving angel, sent by God to let me know that someone cared, that *He* cared."

My mind flashed back to 1979 . . . Montana State Hospital . . . the night Karen became *my* saving angel. *Karen, look what you started!*

The way the Lord used me with Carol was reason enough on its own for me to get out of a sickbed and go to England. Whereas my sicknesses in the past were often a subconscious way to avoid responsibility, when bed had been my hiding place, this is no longer true. I find that life today is exciting. I want to be where the action is. I have discovered the impact of those three words: *Expect the best.*

Something really sparked inside me when I told myself that good was going to happen on this trip to England. Right away my attitude changed from negative to positive.

In fact, I think that is what started the healing process inside me. I was opposing a stronghold of illness in my own body. I had an expectation in my spirit that, yes, the fever and the flu bug could be overcome.

Medication is a factor here, of course. But antibiotics and cold remedies go just so far. After taking them, I would still spend days in bed.

But it was more than medication that sustained me over that 48-hour period.

I know, too, that change began to work inside of me soon after we asked people to pray. For when people pray they use Scripture promises of belief. One of my favorites: ''All things are possible to him who believes'' (Mark 9:23). Prayer changes situations and people.

Does believing in prayer make it come true? Does your expecting the best ensure that it will take place?

Not always, of course, for there is much in the spiritual realm we don't understand. But from now on, when situations arise like the British television invitation, I intend to move ahead with the following steps:

1) Ask God if this is something I should do.
2) If it has His O.K., pray that heavenly forces will clear the way.
3) Then expect the best to happen!

–*12*–

Second Chance

$\mathscr{R}$ECOVERY $\mathscr{P}$RINCIPLE # *12*
Seize the Moment

$\mathscr{A}$fter Len's and my prayer time this morning I looked at myself in the mirror, really looked at myself, with disbelief at the person staring back at me.

Part of me can barely remember, or perhaps chooses not to remember, the Sandy of years ago—bloated from the excesses of alcohol and food, dissipated from the ravages of addiction and excess.

The clear-eyed, slender, gray-haired woman in the mirror is an example of the mercy and grace of God's reconstruction, resurrection power. He does indeed restore the years the locusts have eaten. Not that we don't pay a price for our selfish, sinful behavior. We do. But the God of new beginnings is forgiving. In remaking us, He adds something new and beautiful that was not there before.

He is also the God of the second chance. And the third. Or however many others it takes.

I thought of Lauren, that irrepressible, free spirit who was my friend at the halfway house back in 1981. Still in bondage to alcohol and unhealthy male relationships, Lauren fled the halfway house to marry a man she met in treatment. Since both were in the early recovery stage, neither was ready for marriage and a second chance at a healthy life.

Over the next few years Lauren and I continued a Christmas card friendship. Each year her card came from a different address, indicating that her life was chaotic. I was now married to Len, working with compulsive-addictive people.

One Thanksgiving Lauren's face kept appearing before me. How was she? Sober? Still married to Mark?

The lesson I have learned in recovery when a thought like this comes is, *Seize the moment.* I felt prompted to write Lauren a letter of friendship and encouragement. So I wrote her a short note expressing my concern for her—for her health and healing, for her life with Mark. I sent it off feeling oddly relieved. Her face stopped haunting me.

No Christmas card from her that year. *Probably she moved again, I thought, and didn't get my note.*

The following October I was in Minneapolis for a conference and decided to try to contact Lauren. I got her phone number from Mark's legal secretary after much assurance I was a good friend.

Lauren's voice was crisp and bright on the other side of the phone.

"Oh, Sands, how incredible you would call just now. I have been trying to get in touch with you to tell you what happened. You'll never believe it!

"In August my life was unraveling so badly I just wanted to end it all. My marriage was a mess. I was a mess. One Tuesday morning I decided I didn't want to live anymore. I would take my life that day.

"I headed out the door with a prescription for sleeping pills in my purse. I planned to stop at the drugstore first, then get a bottle of vodka. Then, bye-bye, everybody and everything.

"Monday had been such a horrible day, I hadn't even bothered to pick up the mail in the box by our front door. But just as I was leaving, I noticed a pale blue envelope through the slits in the mailbox. Most of my mail was bills, but the blue envelope intrigued me and made me open the box. It was a note from you—a beautiful note dated last November, *nine months ago!*

"I sat down on the stairs and read it. Sands, your words of love and encouragement spoke life to me. My heart began to beat like crazy. It was as though God was telling me through you how much He loved me. It was incredible.

"I canceled my trip to the drugstore. In fact, I went into the bathroom and tore up the sleeping pill prescription and flushed it down the toilet. When Mark came home from work I told him what happened. We had a good cry and made a commitment to try harder, that we really loved each other and wanted to work on our marriage.

"He's just out of another treatment center and I'm seeing a counselor. Perhaps I'll go back for more help, too. But I just want you to know that your note saved my life. Thanks, Sands. . . ."

Who can explain the delivery of a letter, written in November, arriving in the receiver's mailbox the following August—at just the right time to stop her from an appointment with death? Only the divine Mailman could have made that happen and given Lauren and Mark the basis for a new start in their marriage.

I shuddered to think what would have happened to Lauren if I had not seized that moment to write the letter God had placed on my heart! God is merciful indeed.

Nowhere has His mercy been more evident than with my children. My alcoholism, my driven behavior, my compulsion to escape the home responsibilities of raising my three children robbed me of years of precious time with them.

They were well cared for, I rationalized. We had live-in help much of the time, plus a roster of eager young babysitters anxious to make spending money. Deep in my heart I knew all was not well, that I was violating basic qualities God had placed in me as a woman—as wife, mother, nurturer, keeper of the hearth.

In my creative fantasies I visualized happy hours with my sons and daughter doing wonderfully artistic things. I was always going to build an Indian fort and a doll house, to take them on picnics, to teach them to be creative with paints and glue and crafts.

My feeble attempts always ended in frustration for us all. Alcohol destroys creativity and the patience needed to hang in there with clumsy, small fingers that do not respond easily to adult directions.

One afternoon I did teach all three to sew on buttons. I can still see Brad, Brent and Lisa standing before me—ages eight, nine and ten— their fingers swathed with Band-Aids, clutching ragged squares of material covered with colorful buttons. Some had been sewn on top of each other. Others hung by a thread or two. But the triumphant looks in their eyes stabbed my heart. They had succeeded at doing something with Mom. And for Mom.

Why haven't you been doing things like this all along? I asked myself.

One day after Werner and I had separated, I heard the sewing machine whirring in the next room. Lisa had taught herself to sew by observing me. For hours her young, slender body sat patiently at the old Singer, stitching little purses of fabric. Small squares with foldover tops. She always sewed a snap under the flap to secure it. She made dozens of them in every material imaginable. I would return home and find a fresh stack of her offerings on the foot of my bed or neatly piled on my pillow. Perhaps it was her therapy, a way of escaping the pain and fear in her ten-year-old heart of missing her father and coping with an often-absent mother.

I weep today as I look at a multicolored cotton quilted purse from those dark days. The words *I LOVE YOU* cut out from red felt are pinned to the flap just as they were fashioned almost twenty years ago. My fingers trace the message of love from my child while a deep sense of loss gnaws at my soul. The loss of what I missed. What we all missed. . . .

That is when the words of my faith kick in and I hear God saying, "I will restore the years the locusts have eaten" (see Joel 2:25).

When I married Len in 1985, I inherited six delightful grandchildren ages four months to sixteen years. Clearly a challenge, but more important for me, a second chance! The passage of five years has brought us two more grandchildren. With my own three children, the total of my immediate family reaches 21.

At the end of July our clan gathers at Evergreen Farm for a two-week family time. What a lively, exuberant, heartwarming time it is!

The farmhouse almost explodes with activity. Children's voices and bodies seem to be everywhere. The women cluster in the kitchen organizing meals and housekeeping details. The men plan entertainment and special groundskeeping projects around the farm. And the two cats run for their lives!

On the wall of the kitchen is posted a large yellow cardboard sign with the heading *Camp Evergreen*. Each family member is expected to sign up for one duty a day. It is the only way to handle such a large group of people.

The women sign up for a certain meal and are responsible for shopping and preparing the food. Others are enlisted to set up and clean up afterward. A "kitchen cop" is assigned for each day whose unpopular job it is to see that the kitchen is not a disaster area, that everyone does his or her assigned task.

Mealtimes are marvelous times of fellowship and fun. One outstanding such time was the occasion of Len's seventieth birthday. We decided to have a surprise "Teddy Bear Picnic and Hoedown" to honor the occasion, complete with scores of bears perched in trees, in flowerbeds, hanging from the pale blue umbrella over the food table. They were everywhere.

The entire family marched around the yard to the strains of the "Teddy Bear Picnic," snaking around the patio, past the white brick smokehouse and down the lawn and back to the patio.

Len was presented with a pair of jeans and a straw hat, which he donned good-naturedly for the occasion.

Len's daughters-in-law gave him a T-shirt with a huge black and white Holstein cow on the front—Len likes to call cows poochie-poochies.

"This is a *cow*, Dad," Linda joked. "Not a poochie-poochie. Cows are *not* poochie-poochies."

The entertainment for the evening was a family square dance. We had enough mobile family members for two squares of eight. A square-dance caller and his wife explained patiently the various dance calls and moves. Country music blared over loudspeakers from the front porch. People in cars passing by must have been curious. "Do-si-do, off you go." Right there on the front lawn.

We were convulsed with laughter and excitement. The children loved it as we all became a tangle of arms and legs, sometimes hopping in the right direction, often in the wrong.

As I clapped my hands to the catchy Western tunes, time stopped for a moment. I saw that God was not only restoring me and my children, He was giving me more family. I felt a sense of sacred trust as the matriarch of this beautiful, energetic creative group. He was indeed restoring. Not only restoring, but increasing!

And I was learning to grab hold of these opportunities and make something special of them. The recovery process had relaxed me, slowed down my motor and, most important, given me something new—an inner discernment to know how and when to seize a special moment.

How had this come about?

As I prayed about this, the Lord took me back to my early years and showed me that I always had a flair for remembering friends in small ways, sending them cards with drawings and scribbles. Alcohol had dulled this gift.

But when I became serious about my recovery and stopped abusing my body, I was given a second chance. Creativity returned.

Missed opportunities are still part of my life, of course. Fatigue, an overly heavy schedule or a bout of discouragement will keep me from seizing a special moment. But I am learning to rise above these low points because I want the joy these happenings bring to my spirit.

I have a choice, of course. I can give in to my temporary fatigue or busyness or discouragement and miss a special moment. Or I can choose to reach out for it.

On one rainy August afternoon the children were a bit restless, especially the little girls—Hadley, age six, Mary Catherine, age five, and Whitaker, age three. Suddenly I remembered something I always wished I had done for my daughter, Lisa—a dress-up tea party with hats and flowers and all the trimmings.

I asked Linda and Susan, the girls' mothers, what they thought of the idea. They were wildly enthusiastic, as were the girls.

The next two hours became a time of preparation, a large part of the fun. The girls dressed in their best dresses. I helped out with my treasure trove of fabrics, old jewelry, silk flowers and hats. Each girl was decked out for "high tea" in the most outlandish outfits imaginable.

Hadley selected a headpiece of pink velvet ribbon and hot pink roses and petunias. Mary Catherine wore a long, printed cotton dress with her long hair tied up with navy ribbons and flowers. She carried a fan. Whitaker was dressed in white, a huge white net bow and silver ribbons perched precariously atop her dark hair.

They all wanted several necklaces and rings. And makeup. Each girl wore lipstick, blush, mascara and nail polish—a big treat!

They looked adorable in their finery, preening and posing self-consciously for my camera, a photo opportunity if ever there was one.

I had set a small table on the porch with a lacy white cloth and napkins, fresh flowers in a little crystal vase. Small white demitasse cups with gold trim marked each place. A colorful Miss Piggy teapot added a whimsical touch to the table. Treats included a large plate of cookies and pastel mints.

The girls giggled and sipped and chatted merrily. Linda, Susan and I observed from a distance the little drama before us, cameras clicking: three lovely little girls happily being little girls. There was something innocent and enchanting and nostalgic about it all.

As I watched, a part of me long forgotten was touched at a deep level. It was as though I could see myself with new eyes, eyes of forgiveness. Though I had not done something like this for my own children, God was giving me another chance with other little ones whom I loved, whose lives I could impact.

After dinner, when some rain had stopped, most of the family gathered on the croquet field. I remembered that the tea party table had not been cleared off from the front porch and headed there.

The evening sounds and colors were soft and comforting. Locusts hummed their special song from lush trees bordering the house. Fireflies sparkled tiny yellow greetings on the front lawn. Soon the air would be alive with thousands of little blinking lights.

For a moment I sat in a porch rocker listening to the sounds of a summer night mingled with the excited voices of our competitive family on the croquet field. I stared at the tea party table next to me, the pristine cloth now covered with spills and crumbs and knotted up napkins . . . three small chairs askew . . . flowers wilting in the vase.

Today would always carry for me a special memory, a moment seized and captured on film for generations to come. And perhaps, too, for three little girls.

-13-

Incest Comes Out of the Closet

RECOVERY PRINCIPLE # 13
Forgive Those Who Have Hurt You

---

*W*hen it happened to me at the age of five, I gave myself an order: "I will never tell anyone." A beloved uncle had sexually molested me and I didn't understand anything about it. *Perhaps it's my fault,* I thought. Afterward I kept washing my hands over and over.

As the months and years passed, I tried to forget what Uncle Ralph had done to me when my parents were outside working in the garden. I buried it in my subconscious. Years later while I was attending a compulsivity clinic, the subject of incest came up. I asked the director if this single instance of sexual abuse could be one of the underlying causes of my compulsive behavior.

"Yes," he answered. "Your shame/guilt reaction in this case was a major factor. You felt you couldn't talk to anyone. You tried ritual handwashing to cleanse yourself. You blamed yourself and forced the pain inward. This violation of your personhood seriously damaged not only the trust you had in yourself, but your trust in others. When the boundaries of your world as you knew it were stolen, the door was opened for compulsive-addictive behavior."

During my healing time at the halfway house just outside Minneapolis, I was told that underneath my smiling countenance was deep-rooted anger. So I was assigned "anger work." This meant going back as far as I could remember, noting events and people that made me angry.

Uncle Ralph!

"Go back to that place and that episode," the counselor instructed me. "Tell your uncle how you felt about his abuse of you. You're not a helpless little girl now. Tell him whatever you need to." She gave me several pillows to use.

Closing my eyes for concentration, I went back in time to Uncle Ralph's living room. I could smell the Sir Walter Raleigh tobacco he rolled into homemade cigarettes . . . hear the sound of several clocks ticking from the hallway.

Then I saw Uncle Ralph sitting in his squeaky wooden rocker. Felt his hands on me, heard him wheezing, clicking his teeth. I started to sob and beat my thighs.

"Use the pillows," the counselor ordered.

"I loved and trusted you, Uncle Ralph, and you abused me. I was little and couldn't resist. You hurt me! You scared me! I hate you for that! I hate you! I hate you!"

I was shouting now, my voice high and shrill. The five-year-old Sandy was doubled over, pounding the pillows with both fists.

During those sessions I realized that in the past my anger had erupted all right, only in indirect, inappropriate ways. Example: overeating. You could never have convinced me when I was binging on chocolate that I was really acting out my inner rage. Not just at Uncle Ralph, but at all the times I had swallowed my feelings and said nothing. It made no difference that my dress size was headed for the twenties, that I was totally repulsed at myself and nauseated physically by food. The raging dragon inside demanded to be fed. Or placated with cigarettes. Or booze. Or a new outfit.

The healing therapy I went through regarding Uncle Ralph became part of *The Compulsive Woman*. Soon after its publication in 1987 I received an astonishing letter from Marilyn Van Derbur, Miss America 1958. While traveling with Marilyn when I was a public relations specialist for one of the Miss America Pageant sponsors, we became friends and have kept in touch ever since.

She poured out her heart to me about the incestuous abuse she had received from her father:

Your book brought up such agony for me. You will be able to understand what a difficult journey I have had. I know now why people want to kill themselves—not because they want to die, but because they can't endure the pain one more day.

One of the ways I survived was typing, typing, typing. Sometimes I would type so furiously my fingers would type what my mind couldn't think . . . what my lips couldn't say. I would read what I had written and then just lie on the floor and sob.

I would type and edit. Type and edit. I seemed compelled to try to make sense out of what happened to me on paper. I spent hours doing that.

Without my husband, Larry, I would never even have tried to make it. I always thought I was tough and strong and smart. I found I couldn't control my body or my mind.

I'm so grateful that you found Len and that he found you. I think of you often and smile each time I do. I'm grateful, too, that you have found peace and love. I have had Larry every inch of the way and I am experiencing a peace that is indescribable . . . finally.

Here are excerpts from the "typings" Marilyn included in her letter to me. These typings later became the basis for articles she wrote for major American publications in 1991, drawing national attention to the problem of incest and winning widespread support for the cause she has undertaken of helping incest victims:

My father was powerful, handsome, intelligent and so success-ful that, upon his death in 1984, his obituary ran on the front page of our Denver paper. . . . The F. S. Van Derbur Boy Scout Building was named after him.

My mother and my three older sisters were beautiful and out-

standing in their different ways. How lucky I was to have been born into such a family of influence and affluence. I believed that with every ounce of my being. I had to, because by the time I was seven I was so traumatized I had begun to live in a fantasy world that I had created in order to survive.

My day child, the happiest girl in the world, had already separated from my night child. The two knew nothing of one another. I took my head off my body to live during the day. My body, hopeless and helpless, remained in my bedroom to take the endless degradation and humiliation from my father at night. To use the proper psychiatric term, I dissociated.

The more my nighttime child became ugly, filthy and despicable, the more my daytime child needed to excel in every area of her life. And she/I did! Whether it was in academics (Phi Beta Kappa honors) or sports (U. of Colorado ski team, AAU swim meets) or leadership as a college sophomore (I became Miss

America) or an adult career of speaking to thousands at business and sales meetings (once named "Outstanding Woman Speaker in America"), I was the best!

But for reasons I would not understand until years later, I always felt guilty about the charmed life I had. I would never have survived emotionally or physically if my life had not been blessed by a young man I met when I was fifteen years old —Larry Atler, senior class president in our high school. I fell quickly and completely in love with him. It took me a full year to win his love, but once I did, it was a strong and abiding love that would, in time, teach me how to love, honor and trust again.

A year after her father's death, Marilyn revealed to her mother the sexual abuse she had endured. At first she refused to believe her, until Marilyn's oldest sister, Gwen, also disclosed that she had been victimized by her father.

Then, in an act of unprecedented courage, Marilyn went public with her story, convinced that she was just one of millions of women (and men) damaged by incest. The result: Marilyn has a national ministry to these people. In the Denver area she, with the Kempe National Center, formed a support group called Survivors United Network. More than 2,000 people are now involved.

The major point Marilyn makes: *Incest victims do not get healed until they go back in time to the abuse, face up to what really happened and work through it with professional counseling.*

The wounds of incest go deep. During every workshop or talk I give in which I mention my own molestation, women line up afterward to confide (often for the first time) their experiences. I suggest they go to support groups, seek professional counseling. In addition, I pray with them for God to heal them at a deep level.

Some of my most memorable encounters have taken place at the Aqueduct Conference Center outside of Chapel Hill, North Carolina. I have been there three times with Len and David Hazard to lead writers' workshops, and also with Edith Marshall, a psychotherapist in Chatham, Massachusetts, and daughter-in-law of the late Catherine Marshall LeSourd. Edith's sparkle, warmth and expertise win friends for her wherever she goes. With her I have done three weekend workshops on the general theme of overcoming compulsive behavior and finding healing and wholeness and freedom.

As soon as you arrive at Aqueduct, something in the quiet peace starts the healing process. The main building resembles a classic ski chalet with its ceiling-to-floor plate glass windows. In the lobby a long, hand-carved mahogany buffet holds conference literature and always a large basket of shiny red apples—a lovely touch of ambiance for the hungry traveler or conferee with a terminal case of the munchies.

To the left is a small chapel/counseling room decorated tastefully with antiques and brass lamps and Oriental rugs. At one end is a velvet-covered kneeling bench for prayer and meditation; a small rose love seat and chair grace the other end.

The central meeting room at Aqueduct looks, again, like the living room of a beautiful ski lodge. At one end is a massive gray flagstone fireplace with a raised hearth. In the center of the room are two light gray sofas arranged in a "U."

Aqueduct's host, Tommy Tyson, is a big teddy bear of a man with a booming voice, an infectious smile and vast experience as a teacher and pastor. His son Tom not only has many of his father's hospitality and teaching skills, but is an accomplished musician, especially on the piano, and manages the center with flair and skill.

On this particular Thursday night through Sunday noon conference, Edith and I began with a "Getting to Know You" evening. To set the theme we wore our *It's Never Too Late to Have a Happy Childhood* T-shirts with white slacks.

We told the women we wanted to dig deeply into women's issues, that our objective was to help them find freedom from any bondages they had arrived with. Many women smiled optimistically; others were wistful. Some were frozen-faced, probably with years and years of deep hurt.

Once Edith and I began with our own hurtful experiences, the women felt freer to open up and bear their hearts to the group. We asked that the confidentiality principle practiced in twelve-step recovery groups be in effect for the weekend. There were obvious sighs of relief.

Julie, a frail wisp of a young woman from the Northeast with whom I bonded one night at dinner, was one of the first to report her incest experience. She revealed at that evening's meeting that her father had molested her for over eight years. She suspected the abuse had started before that, when she was an infant.

Her warm brown eyes filled with tears and her face contorted in anger as she said, "My mother knew what was going on with Dad and me. And she never said anything. She never did anything to protect me. I can't forgive her for that.

"She always played the helpless one, the one who needed to be taken care of. She expected me to meet her needs when I was dying inside. She never could see my pain." Julie sobbed into the wad of tissues in her hand.

"I don't know why I've said all of this. But I've been sitting on this pain for so long, I can't stand another minute."

Just before the evening meeting broke up, Edith looked at Julie. "I have the feeling that you very much need one of the older women here to pray with you and tuck you into bed. You need a mother tonight to care for you and be with you. Does that sound silly to you, Julie?"

Julie's face exploded in a smile. "I'd like that very much. And I'd like Sandy to be my mother."

"O.K., then, you two take off."

As Julie and I walked down the winding path to her lodge, I knew this was to be a new experience for both of us. In a way, an adventure. I sensed that her trust in me had grown during the evening.

Lord, I prayed silently, *please be with both of us. You be the counselor by giving me just the right words to say.*

We entered a spacious wooden building serving as a dormitory and headed up the thickly carpeted stairs to her room on the second floor. The halls were silent now since we had arrived before the others. The whole building had a quiet, almost holy atmosphere.

The woman who was to be Julie's roommate had canceled at the last minute, so Julie had a private room.

She settled herself into a straight chair next to the dresser. Her tiny body looked almost childlike as she folded her hands in her lap and crossed her feet neatly, like a prim and proper little girl at a dance recital. Her soft brown eyes searched mine expectantly.

"Julie, let's start by doing some role-playing. I'll be your mother. You speak to me as though you were speaking to her. And don't hold back. Let it fly! Nothing you say will shock me or make me judge you or will cause me to flee. I'm here for as long as this takes. I don't have anything to do until breakfast at eight tomorrow morning."

After I pulled up another chair and sat directly in front of Julie, she began self-consciously, her voice cracking with emotion.

"Mother, *where were you?* Where were you all the times Daddy came into my bedroom, or when I was in the bathtub, or wherever I was that he got to me? Why, why, why didn't you help me? Rescue me? You knew what was going on. I could tell by the funny way you looked at me . . . almost like I was competition for you for Daddy's love, like I was a grown woman or something sick like that. You had to know even if you pretended you didn't. I was so little and so frightened and you never once came into my room and comforted me.

"Sometimes I heard your satin bathrobe rustling down the hall. You were listening, weren't you? *Weren't you?* And I hate you for that. I hate you! Why didn't you help me? Why did you let me suffer all those years?"

Julie was screaming now. The veins on her neck were bulging in rage. She was spitting out the words in my face, totally absorbed in the emotion of the minute. She started to shake. Her eyes were closed. Her body pitched backward. Her head hit the wall with a thud.

What is happening? I thought to myself. *I hope I'm not in over my head.*

Julie regained her composure briefly, hung her head and started to sob and heave. Her jeans soon were marked with tears.

My mind was racing. *Lord, give me the words her mother might have said to her that would comfort her and make her feel safe and valuable as a child.*

"Julie," I began, "you are right. I did know. I wanted to help you, to reach out to you and comfort you, but I couldn't. Your father terrified me with his violent temper, his threats to kill us all. There were many nights when he returned from your room that I wanted to stab him or shoot him, but I couldn't go through with it. I was too scared.

"Often I'd be there outside your room just to make sure he wasn't killing you or suffocating you. I didn't know what he would do to you. I felt powerless to stop him. He was so much like your grandfather. I was scared of him, too. Grampa did to me what your father has done to you. I've been an incest victim, too. I've never been able to deal with the trauma of my own childhood. And when the same things were happening to you, it was like your grampa was doing it all over again to me. And I felt small and helpless and terrified.

"That doesn't excuse me, sweetheart, for just standing by while you were being victimized, but perhaps it will help you to understand better why I was so paralyzed. I couldn't protect you. I couldn't even protect myself. Do you understand?

"Oh, Julie, can you ever forgive me? I am so sorry for what's happened to you, that I wasn't there for you. This awful secret has just about driven me crazy. Please, please forgive me. I'm so sorry I've hurt you and let you down. Please?" I was crying now, too.

Julie's brown eyes were shut tight in anguish, her mouth contorted in bitterness.

"Oh, Mother, everything in me wants to say no, I won't forgive you, but I know I must. Though my heart can't say I forgive you, I know I must *will* to forgive you. Yes, I will to forgive you. I'll have to trust God that He will make it real. That I'll have the feelings of forgiveness. But honestly, right now I don't have them. I wish I did, but I can't just manufacture them. I want to forgive you. I really *want* to."

I held the small, sobbing body in my arms for a long time. Julie wept convulsively, wetting the shoulder of my sweater through to the skin.

At some deep level I was being healed, too. Forgiveness for my uncle who had molested me when I was five solidified at a deeper level. I felt freer and more cleansed through the pain of Julie's experience. My situation was much less traumatic than her years of abuse. I suddenly felt very thankful and relieved and grateful.

We broke from the embrace and Julie reached for a wad of tissues she had jammed into the back pocket of her jeans. She blew her nose enthusiastically again and again. A triumphant smile crossed her pale face.

"Whew! I'm glad that's over. I feel so much better. I really do. Thanks, Sandy, for being here. And by the way, how did you know my mother was an incest victim, too? She confessed it to me just recently."

I was taken aback by what she said. How *had* I known?

"The Holy Spirit told me," I replied.

Julie emerged from the bathroom in a long white flannel nightgown ready for bed. She eased herself between the covers and pulled the blankets up to her neck. Only her head was peeking out. She looked so young, so little. I fluffed her pillow, making a nest around her head. She closed her eyes. A serene smile crept across her lips—a little girl's smile. A secure little girl's smile.

I sat down on the bed and stroked her forehead.

"I love you, Julie," I said as her mother would have said. "I'm sorry I wasn't there to tuck you in all the years you needed me, but I'm here now. I want you to know how very much I love you. How precious and special you are to me. Rest now, little one, and know you are safe and secure and loved very deeply."

Next I led Julie in "Now I lay me down to sleep" and the Lord's Prayer. I sang a little lullaby to her. Her breathing became regular. Deep. I knew she had drifted off to sleep. Then I stole from the room quietly, closing the door behind me.

The memory of Julie's peaceful, beautiful face stayed with me as I walked the short distance through the damp, pungent night air to the main lodge and to my room. And I carried Julie in my heart long after the Aqueduct conference ended. Sharing such anguish and joy had bonded us as spiritual mother and daughter.

Some weeks later this letter came from Julie:

Dear Sandy,

Because you ministered so lovingly to me at the conference, I have been praying for you ever since. The result—I have been shown a picture of the woundedness still in your heart.

Then came another picture, that of the woman caught in adultery waiting to be stoned by the crowd. In prayer, I saw all those accusers of 2,000 years ago standing with rocks in their hands ready to throw them at her. Suddenly your face was the face of every person in that crowd. One of self-hatred, another of self-condemnation, another of guilt, pain, anger, judgment, despair.

Then each one of those Sandys came forward and put down her rock into a basket at the feet of Jesus, and quietly walked away.

And you, the one "caught in sin" and filled with such pain, stood alone before the Lord. He looked into your tear-filled eyes and said with unfathomable kindness and tenderness, "Neither do I condemn you."

Sandy, I don't think you "goofed" when you said in your closing talk that the Lord was going to give you back diamonds.

I see Jesus, Sandy, back in that scene with you, picking up that basket filled with all those stones. Jesus lifts it up toward the Father and, as He prays, a shaft of brilliant white light shines down from heaven directly upon the stones, and they are transformed into many sparkling diamonds.

The rock labeled *self-condemnation* is turned into diamonds of mercy and compassion.

The rock of *guilt* becomes purity of heart and self-control.

The rock of *pain* becomes a diamond of healing grace.

Anger is changed into peace.

Judgment becomes forgiveness.

The rock of *despair* becomes diamonds of joy, hope, patience and trust.

Then the Lord lowers the basket. He looks into your eyes with great love and, reaching into the basket, pulls out a beautiful, sparkling necklace made of all these diamonds. They are strung together on a cord of God's love that can never be broken. Jesus puts this necklace on you, and as He does so, a shaft of light, His healing and transforming light, travels from each diamond into your heart, wherein the graces of the Spirit represented by each diamond will always be.

You kneel before Him, thanking Him, and He blesses you.

Healing the wounds of incest take time. If you are an incest victim I suggest the following procedure:

1) If the experience is buried deeply in your subconscious, go back in time, asking God to reveal to you what He wants you to see. Then let the pain of it come forth. Draw it up from your depths and face it. Healing won't start until you do.

2) Find someone to help you. A qualified counselor sympathetic to your faith is my recommendation. Don't try to do it by yourself. You need someone with experience to work with you.

3) Forgive the person or persons involved. This may take time and you will probably need help to do it. But forgiving the abuser is the key to your freedom and recovery.

4) Focus on this truth: God is the Healer. He loves you and wants you restored to healthy, joyful living.

−14−

The Conspiracy of Silence

$\mathscr{R}$ECOVERY $\mathscr{P}$RINCIPLE # 14
Talk About It

$\mathcal{I}$ have often wished our family had been able to communicate at a deeper level. The weather was always a safe subject. When asked, everyone was always "Fine, thank you." (Horrors that one would admit to physical weakness!) Superficial, non-confrontational subjects were O.K., but I got the message at an early age that serious subjects or topics that touched on personal issues were *verboten*. We were not to talk about them.

A dome of quiet would descend over our home should feelings get out of hand or an unpleasant subject come up. I used to wonder why we couldn't talk about certain things, but I learned to keep my mouth shut. I didn't get into trouble that way.

Nowhere is the conspiracy of silence more obvious than in the area of sexuality. Why is sex so hard to talk about in a family? My mother didn't tell me the facts of life. Her mother didn't tell her. And to my deep regret, I didn't tell my daughter—or sons, for that matter. They learned about sex from their peers.

As children, my friend of many years, Betty Lou, and I used to make drawings of boys and girls, scribbling in what we *thought* men's sex organs looked like. In retrospect the results were pretty hysterical. We giggled and tittered nervously for fear someone would catch us in this forbidden speculation.

Back in the '40s, especially in a little Vermont town, no one talked openly about sex. Once I saw our neighbor, Mr. Grant, frantically hosing down two dogs on his lawn who were locked in *l'amour*. He was so embarrassed he kept his back to me, muttering about "damn dogs in heat." I thought he was referring to the steamy August afternoon.

At dinner that evening I reported the afternoon adventures of the dogs next door to my assembled grandparents and aunts and uncles. I couldn't understand the sudden silence around the table, why some dove for their water glasses and napkins while my grandmother, red-faced, headed for the pantry. Absentminded, too, for she returned moments later without whatever it was she had jumped up to get.

The bathroom on the first floor of our St. Johnsbury Center home was just off the kitchen. On the rim of the large claw-footed bathtub, just peeking out from behind the white tieback curtains, a mysterious cobalt-blue box appeared and disappeared regularly. The white letters on the side of the box spelled *K O T E X. What a funny name!* I thought to myself. And under the delicate, stilt-like logo were inscribed the words *Sanitary Napkins*.

Those must be very special napkins, I decided. But why were they in the bathroom and not in the kitchen cupboard?

One day I asked my mother, "What are Kotex, Mummy? What are we saving them for?"

She got flustered. "I'll—er, er, er—tell you about them when it's time."

All this delaying tactic did, of course, was to further pique my curiosity. Kotex took on a mystery as deep and dark as the box in which they were stored.

I was haunted by *When it's time*.

Time for what?

Why had mother blushed so?

And why wouldn't Gram explain, either? She had gotten that "I think I've just smelled ammonia'' look on her face and changed the subject.

Nor was my Aunt Ethel much help.

Nor my Aunt Dorothy.

They both smiled knowingly and looked away at some fly speck on the ceiling. Aunt Dorothy actually snickered out loud.

Was there anything funny about these little white gauze-covered pads?

One day I took one out of the box. What a peculiar, narrow shape it had! What a cute little doll mattress this would make! I could see why they were called ''sanitary.'' They were even whiter than Gram's sheets, and that was saying a lot. My grandmother had the whitest sheets on any clothesline in St. Johnsbury Center.

One Sunday evening, as parishioners of the Congregational church, it was our family's turn to host our young pastor, Mr. Cushman, and his lovely bride of six months.

Great care and thought had gone into preparing a succulent baked ham. The scalloped potatoes were browned to perfection. Green beans picked fresh from the garden. A glistening strawberry Jello salad bursting with fruit cocktail. Homemade Parker House rolls. And Gram's famous raspberry-filled sugar cookies.

As family and guests took their places in the dining room, I was helping Mother with last-minute table settings when I realized she was going to be one napkin short. And it was at the pastor's place.

"Wait a minute, Mummy," I cried triumphantly. "I'll get a napkin for you."

Racing to the bathroom, I prayed that the cobalt-blue box would be on the back of the bathtub. It was! My heart raced with excitement. Who more than the pastor deserved the best napkin in the house?

Bursting back into the dining room, I headed for the pastor, now seated at the table and taking his first sip of iced tea. He saw me coming, waving the Kotex in the air by its gauze tab.

"Here, Mummy!" I crowed, relishing the knowledge that I had rescued the moment. "Here's a sanitary napkin for Pastor Cushman."

The iced tea in the pastor's mouth exploded in a stream.

Looks of shock. And disbelief.

Uncle Sam buried his face in his napkin.

Aunt Dorothy choked down a laugh.

My mother rolled her eyes heavenward and grabbed the back of Aunt Ethel's chair.

And my grandmother made another impromptu dash for the pantry.

It was years before I understood why no one ever thanked me for my clever solution to the napkin problem.

In fact, that evening was always referred to as *"that"* night when Pastor and Mrs. Cushman came to dinner. . . .

As I look back on our life in Vermont forty years ago, I can see a lot of things wrong about the conspiracy of silence in our family. Children learned about sex in an unhealthy way, whereas frank mother-daughter or father-son conversations would have cleared up a lot of confusion.

The conspiracy of silence in a family like Julie's, the young woman at the Aqueduct conference, allowed abusive incest to continue for years, seriously damaging all the parties involved. Such silence protected the course of infidelity, promoted distrust, resentment, pain.

In fact, this scenario is played over and over in millions of homes year after year, generation after generation. The three laws springing out of this conspiracy: *Don't talk. Don't trust. Don't feel.*

Yet the other extreme, which we have today care of the sexual revolution, is equally destructive. The new openness and frankness, which could be healthy, has led to a loosening of almost all barriers. As a result, free sex today is an untamed monster, destroying homes and damaging lives just as drugs do. Most people today consider affairs and adultery acceptable. The *f* word is said over and over in films, plays and conversations.

142

One of the worst results? Sex has become so talked about, so examined on television and in the movies, that it has become commonplace. The mystery is gone. And it often ends up being, well, boring. Ask a dozen women how they feel about sex, as I did recently. Most actually said, "I can live without it."

Children today know a great deal about sex as soon as they enter school. Where do they learn? Not usually from parents but from peers. Or from pornographic magazines and films.

Suddenly I have a warm, nostalgic feeling about my own childhood and the confusion I encountered with adults about sex. Their embarrassment made sex and the changes a woman's body went through seem mysterious and romantic and important.

If the long-ago conspiracy of silence in homes was wrong, and equally so the unbridled sexual revolution of today, what is the answer?

I have found the answer through readings and teachings on sexuality for Christians, and through the following principles, which I have been grappling with for a dozen years or more:

1) *Openness.* Support groups have helped me here as we share our pain, our experiences, our strength and our hopes.
2) *Trust.* For me, this began with a commitment to God. When I could trust Him, I could begin to trust people. And myself.
3) *Talking about it.* Learning to discuss sex in a healthy way has not taken away the mystery of it, but given me an infinite respect for the power and sacredness God meant it to have. Talking about sex openly with my children has lifted the code of silence in our family and opened the way for new honesty and healing among us.

– 15 –

Birthday Party Therapy

RECOVERY PRINCIPLE # 15
Celebrate

The wording on the T-shirts that Edith Marshall and I like to wear when we minister to women has proven magnificently true: *It's Never Too Late to Have a Happy Childhood.*

True—and vitally important. There is great healing power in child-like joy and abandon. Thinking back to my own childhood, I am only too aware of how unacceptable it was in many of our families of origin to be either childlike or joyful.

Discovering one's lost childhood usually starts with the peeling away of layers and layers of hurt, abuse and trauma. It doesn't happen instantly. It took me several years to locate my inner child deep within the recesses of my subconscious. Inviting this child in me, and also in others, to come out and play has been exciting and deeply fulfilling.

My first experience with what I call "birthday party therapy" occurred several years ago at Evergreen Farm. Ellen, a good friend, was turning fifty, a birthday many women fear and dread.

I had known Ellen through prayer conferences in the Washington, D.C., area. News of the suicide of her beautiful daughter, Amy, at age eighteen had come to our Breakthrough intercession ministry months before in the form of a prayer request for strength for the family to endure this tragic loss. Ellen, her husband (from whom she was separated) and her son were devastated.

Somewhere along the way I learned that Ellen had been reared in a series of orphanages. She had never even had a birthday party. So some of us at Evergreen set about to rectify that with a fiftieth birthday extravaganza—an irresistible challenge for us compulsive women!

First, a trip to the toy department of the local drugstore. Our car's back seat bulged with paper bags: a soft brown teddy bear, a jump rope, a set of jacks, paper dolls, coloring book and crayons, puzzles, pinwheels, pickup sticks, checkers, a bag of marbles, a bottle of liquid soap bubbles, a makeup set with mirror, perfume and lipstick.

We got party hats, nut cups, Mickey Mouse plates and napkins, yards and yards of crepe paper streamers. Balloons and more balloons.

On the day of the party we hung a huge sign on the front door: *Happy 50th, Ellen.* Everywhere there were dolls and teddy bears. The table was a riot of flowers and confetti and favors. Tied to Ellen's chair was a bouquet of helium-filled birthday balloons.

The walls were decorated with *Happy Birthday* banners. Candles winked cheerily from wall sconces and candelabra on the buffet and dining room table. Ellen's gifts were placed in an ornately decorated bushel basket and set on her chair. The scene was outrageously festive.

When Ellen arrived accompanied by her handsome son, Mark, a college senior, her face exploded in joy and wonder and tears of unbelief over what had been prepared for her, and that a dozen friends would come to celebrate the occasion.

It had been fun for me, too. The compulsive quality in me that had for years focused on parties dominated by alcohol had been converted into something constructive, such as family birthday parties, household decorations, picnics for family and friends.

Now it was almost as though the Lord was saying to me, "You will be the instrument I have chosen to restore a sense of worth to Ellen so that she might catch a glimpse of how much I love her and how special she is."

As she sat down gingerly at her seat of honor trying to digest everything around her, Ellen's lovely face seemed to lose 45 years. It was the child inside her who opened the many cards and presents.

Later, Mark and the rest of us carried gifts, games, streamers and balloons to Ellen's station wagon. Ellen was still wearing her metallic red birthday hat. Confetti dotted her hair. Before getting into the car she pulled me aside.

"Sandy, there are just no words to tell you what is in my heart right now. I feel recreated and appreciated and loved. Special. I'm so glad, too, that Mark got to see a side of his mother he never knew existed. For the first time he saw the joyful, happy little girl I didn't know was inside me either, instead of the morose, weeping mother I've been for so long. For I want you to know that I do feel like a little girl. A special little girl.

"You should know something else. Today would have been Amy's birthday, too. Her twentieth." Ellen's eyes filled with tears. "She was born on my thirtieth birthday. And now here's something I want you to have."

She opened the back door of the car and retrieved an object from a shopping bag she had brought from home. Then she presented me triumphantly with a beautiful gray and silver tapestry teddy bear with golden eyes.

"This belonged to Amy. Knowing how you love bears, I want you to have it. It was her favorite. She had quite a collection." Her voice trailed off.

I accepted the bear, deeply touched.

"Amy loved Catherine Marshall's books," Ellen continued. "One of her dreams was to visit Evergreen. She never made it here, but I can't believe today was a coincidence. How thrilled she would have been by all this!"

"Now her bear will be a resident here," I added. "So Amy will be part of Evergreen Farm, too."

I waved goodbye to Ellen and Mark as their station wagon headed up the driveway, thinking, *Lord, You are indeed the Comforter and Healer. The passing years are surely no barrier to You as You help us rediscover our childhoods.*

* * *

While leading a four-day workshop at Aqueduct Conference Center on the subject "Healing the Inner Child," Edith and I decided to try the birthday party therapy on Saturday night. The forty women attending were from 16 to 75, black and white, wealthy and poor. By Saturday evening they had received much teaching on wounded families, lost childhoods, compulsive behavior and generational patterns. We ended with this powerful prayer for the wounded inner child:

Heavenly Father, I come to You as a little child. Wounded. Abandoned. Rejected by important figures early in my life. I am afraid to trust and, I'm ashamed to say, afraid to trust You totally, Lord.

My inner child cries out to You from her dark hiding place. Weeping for what never was. My inner child hides, afraid to be hurt again. I need Your love, Your solace to give me courage to walk into the light.

If I did not have a mother's love, please send the Holy Spirit to hold me close, to rock me, to tell me stories, to fill in the empty parts of me that needed the comfort and warmth only a mother can give.

If I was deprived of a father's love and did not feel that I was wanted, I ask You to hold me, Lord, and let me feel Your strong, protective arms around me.

Walk through my life, Lord, and comfort me when others were not kind.

Heal the wounds of encounters that left me frightened . . . the person who disappointed me . . . the one who was cruel to me . . . the one who was insensitive to my feelings . . . the brother or sister who was preferred . . . my spouse or former spouse . . . any other family member who hurt me . . . the authority figure . . . anyone who wounded me physically, emotionally, sexually, spiritually . . . anyone who caused me to retreat into myself and erect barriers to You or to other people.

If I have felt unwanted, grant me through Your healing love a new sense of worth as a person.

Lord God, by the power of Your Spirit, help me to make a

friend—namely myself. Empower me to forgive myself for my past failures, my mistakes, my moments of weakness and self-ishness, my refusal to forgive myself, my self-hatred and self-loathing.

Help me to see myself as Your precious little girl, the apple of Your eye. May the reality of Your unconditional love be burned deeply into my spirit that I might be set free. To laugh. To play. To skip through a mud puddle . . . knowing my heavenly Father watches with delight.

How great it is, Lord, to feel safe in Your arms, to be able to trust, to be nurtured! And forgiven.

Thank You for drying my tears. For Your promise to restore the years the locusts have devoured.

Many of the women were now sobbing. Others reached out to hold the more distraught. Healing and love were flowing in a mighty way around the room.

Edith was comforting a particularly upset young woman. I marveled at Edith, the nurturer. So gentle. So wise. So caring. So gifted.

As the women regained their composure, I gathered them together.

"Tonight is a very special occasion. Special because we're all going to celebrate our birthdays! Regardless of what date yours is, tonight is going to be a celebration that we are women, that we are chosen and loved by our heavenly Father, that we are Daddy's little girls."

Edith started the tape *Celebration*. As the bouncy beat of the music caught us up in its infectious enthusiasm, the women started to clap their hands. Some began to dance.

Stashed behind one of the couches were two enormous bags of decorations and goodies. Pat Johnson, the Aqueduct office manager, and I had gone shopping for these surprises the day before. Now Pat burst into the room with fifty multicolored, helium-filled balloons. All the women were now in motion, laughing, singing. Some draped themselves with crepe paper streamers, tying them around their heads, waists, wrists or ankles. Others began blowing bubbles or skipping rope. Several women pranced about in a conga line doing Rockette kicks to the music.

Each woman was given a large plastic ring—Minnie or Mickey Mouse, Daisy or Donald Duck. One young woman attached her ring to her nose, to squeals of delight. Another took the little yellow felt hat off the Paddington bear she was carrying and attached it to her long blonde hair with bobby pins. What a picture of sheer delight, this lovely woman with a tiny yellow hat perched on her head, blowing hard on a pink metallic pinwheel, returning to the joyous little girl she had left behind twenty years before.

The noise level by now was deafening with the laughing and shrieking and shouts of glee. Pat looked at me with excited eyes. "Aqueduct has *never* seen anything like this before!" A short while later she returned with a large tray of chocolate cupcakes, each decorated with a candle. She and Edith arranged them on the coffee table in the center of the room.

"O.K., everybody," Edith hollered. "Pick up your birthday cake and come blow out your candle."

All forty of us clustered around the low table to sing "Happy Birthday" to ourselves. Forty voices blended in harmony. There was something almost angelic about each face as it was reflected in the candle glow—forty little girls rejoicing that they were little girls. And—for that moment, anyway—glad that they had been born. Pain, depression and darkness had been banished from our celebration. Only joy and acceptance and love were admitted here.

Then Edith announced it was game time. Cheers! Teams were drawn up; the under-35s against the over-35s for a lively session of charades.

At 11:30 P.M. we called it a night. As the women wandered off to their rooms, chatting happily, Edith and I collapsed on one of the large gray sofas, our feet propped on the coffee table.

"Well, Sandy, I don't know about you, but I had the time of my life," she yawned, a large blue crepe paper bow still draped over her forehead covering one of her eyes.

"Edith, you look ridiculously adorable."

But Edith had actually fallen asleep with a beautiful little smile.

Sunday morning was awards time, to recognize outstanding performances of the night before. To pretty blonde Ann went the prize for the limbo contest, a dance done in the Caribbean in which you slide under a pole that is lowered steadily until there is hardly room for a human form to pass under it.

The Mouseketeer Party Organizer Award went to Lottie, a vivacious redhead from Atlanta. Next, the drawing for a special teddy bear. With great fanfare, Edith drew a name from the box. "And the winner is—Rosemary!"

Rosemary was our oldest conferee who had come with many needs and hurts. The first evening she had sat stonily in her chair as the others shared. Slowly she opened up as the weekend progressed. The evening before she had stood arm in arm with her daughter, her Minnie Mouse ring reflecting the glow of the candle on her cupcake, her lovely face a wreath of smiles. What a contrast to the woman who had arrived! Rosemary had found the little girl within.

Slowly she came forward to receive the little gray teddy. She pressed the small bear to her chest and said, with tears misting behind her glasses, "I've never won anything before in my life."

As I looked at the balloons gathered into an enormous bouquet on the fireplace mantel, I marveled once again at how God had used a birthday party—this time to transform a group of forty women for a few shining moments into that magical place of childhood where joy can take root in the soul, no matter what the date on the calendar.

My recovery continues through workshops on compulsive behavior as I learn through reaching out to others. The birthday celebration helped me discover my own inner child who got lost years ago in the trauma of a dysfunctional home. In the process I see some of the steps[*] compulsive/addictive people like me—and there are millions of us—need to take to get well:

1) *Recognizing* that back there at an early age the natural progression of your childhood was stopped because of a sudden grief, family rupture, physical illness or some other deeply painful event. Because of this, your emotional growth was stunted and your behavior became erratic. Alcoholism or drug abuse, another type of compulsive behavior or a combination thereof tended to follow.

2) *Making contact* with that lost inner child. This can be done in a number of ways. Celebrating the discovery of the lost child is one, as I have done through the birthday party therapy. John Bradshaw suggests "embracing your lost inner child" through meditation.[*] This procedure involves *relaxing* the body; *breathing* exercises; *going back* in time to age seven or before; *walking down* the street to your house; *watching* the small child (you) coming out the front door; *walking up* to this child and telling him or her that you are his or her future; *asking him or her* to go home with you, then taking his/her hand; *turning the corner* to meet your cherished friends and Higher Power (God) waiting to greet you and embrace you.

3) *Being liberated,* which happens when you recognize the need to go back to your childhood, meet the lost child and set her

* John Bradshaw, *Reclaiming the Inner Child* (Los Angeles: Jeremy P. Tarcher, Inc., 1990).

free. Reconnecting with the inner child then enables you to discover your true self.

The above steps are not, of course, a substitution for twelve-step programs and related support groups that over the years have proven their value to the recovery process.

– 16 –

"Sandy, I Hated Your Book"

RECOVERY PRINCIPLE # 16
Be Honest

Those of us in bondage to an addiction create a web of lies to protect ourselves. In time we come to the point at which we believe that these lies are truth; we live in delusion in order to feel good about ourselves. Sometimes we revise and rewrite our personal histories to excuse the shameful things we have done.

To move ahead with recovery, we must face up to our dishonesty and set the record straight whenever possible, even if it means painful confession and confrontation.

In speaking to groups I feel it is essential to be open, vulnerable and as honest as I can. Sometimes the results almost blow me away.

Like the Compulsive Woman Workshop we held in May 1990 at a church in Silver Spring, Maryland. Tina Haroldson, a lovely young woman from the Midwest, is a gifted soloist and provided our special music. Tina's mother was in the audience. Both were close friends of Dottie Schmitt, the pastor's wife, who was a co-speaker.

I had shared my personal story in the morning. The workshop was due to end with my giving a final teaching session on Saturday afternoon. Tina opened this session with a song in her strong soprano; her high notes were so penetrating that I expected the stained glass windows in the sanctuary to pop out. Then Tina drew a deep breath and prepared, we assumed, to give us a final song.

Instead, she turned her gaze to me where I was sitting in the front row. "Sandy, I read your book last year. And I just want you to know I hated it. Hated it because you were so honest. And I felt so convicted."

Tina stooped down for a moment and pulled off the high-heeled black pumps she had been wearing all day, giving herself in the process an aura of vulnerability and realness. I was intrigued that she was allowing herself to do what most people do when their feet hurt. Rarely do entertainers allow themselves this privilege while in front of an audience!

"You didn't write very much about my situation, Sandy." Her voice faltered for a moment. "I have a condition called obsessive-compulsive behavior. My particular problem is that I can't stop pulling out my hair."

There was shocked silence throughout the church. Two hundred women leaned forward, unable to believe the startling confession they were hearing.

None of us, looking at Tina, saw any evidence of a hair-pulling problem. Her carefully coiffed short brown hair was glossy and well-groomed, a fringe of bangs dusting her forehead.

No one was prepared for what happened next.

Carefully Tina placed the microphone back into its stand. Her right hand reached up under her bangs and she proceeded to remove a wig, placing it gently onto the lucite pulpit in front of her. It looked like a small, soft brown puppy curled up asleep next to her Bible.

Gasps of shock and disbelief. Here stood a beautiful young woman beneath an enormous stained glass window, stocking-footed, revealing her deepest, darkest secret to two hundred strangers. Tina's scalp glistened between wispy rows of thin, brown hair. It looked as though she had deliberately and neatly plucked out rows of hair the way a farmer would harvest rows of corn.

Suddenly, from the back of the church, Tina's mother raced down the aisle and up the carpeted steps to the pulpit where her daughter stood. She was in her stocking feet, too.

The two locked in an embrace, their bodies swaying as they wept in each other's arms. We were all weeping.

Mother and daughter broke from the embrace, and Tina reached for the microphone. Her final vocal tribute: "In Heaven's Eyes There Are No Losers."

Though her bald scalp shone under the bright overhead spotlights, on her face was the most radiant expression of peace. Tina's act had freed something inside her. The secret she had covered for so many years was out in the open at last. The Lord had given her courage to reach down into the darkness of her addiction and lift it into the dazzling light of His love.

She sang like an angel. She looked like an angel. I wondered for a moment if she *was* an angel who had been sent to us to show us how painful honesty and humility could set us all free.

We were all on our feet. We cheered. We danced in the aisles. Tina's moment of courage had, in different ways, set us all free.

Afterward Tina picked up her wig, seemingly nonchalant, hugged those of us in the front row and took her seat. I stepped up to the lectern to give the message.

The Spirit of the Lord was almost suffocating in His sweet power in that moment as I looked out at the tear-stained faces.

All I could do was weep into the microphone. No words came out, only the sounds of my sobs. The most eloquent teaching had already been given.

Fourteen months later I received a letter from Tina, along with a report she had sent out to followers of her singing and speaking ministry. Here are excerpts:

Since the age of twelve I have been in bondage to a form of obsessive-compulsive disorder (OCD) called trichatillamania. A person with this disorder has the strange desire to pull out his or her hair. For me the disorder became so uncontrollable that I eventually pulled out all the hair on top of my head and thus had to wear a wig.

Worse than the inconvenience of wearing a hairpiece was the feeling that I was a failure as a Christian. I had prayed and trusted and hoped, but nothing changed. In May 1990 I was in bondage and out of hope.

That May I was invited to Immanuel Church in Silver Spring, Maryland, for a women's weekend retreat. I was preparing to sing two songs when I sensed the Lord speaking to me: *Tina, I want you to tell these ladies about your affliction and then I want you to take off your wig.*

My heart began to race. ''No, Lord, they will think I have no faith.''

But the Lord repeated the requests.

''How could You ask me to do such a thing?'' I implored. ''Why would You require me to face such pain, embarrassment and rejection?''

I decided I just could not do it.

Then Sandy LeSourd spoke. She was so transparent and willing to be real in her talk that my heart was touched. When it was time for me to sing, I knew I had to trust the Lord and be obedient.

When I removed my wig, I felt vulnerable and yet safe, transparent yet accepted, frightened and yet strangely free.

In Jeremiah 24:6-7 God has this promise to anyone who struggles with insecurity: ''I will build them up and not tear them down; I will plant them and not uproot them. I will give them a heart to know me, that I am the Lord. They will be my people, and I will be their God, for they will return to me with all their heart'' (NIV).

The Lord built me up because I had trusted Him enough to be obedient. From the time I took off my wig before those women, I have experienced complete deliverance from trichatillamania. Fourteen months later I was back singing in Immanuel Church. The tears rolled down my face on that morning of July 21, 1991, as I looked out across the congregation. Every person that Sunday morning was standing and praising the Lord for His faithfulness.

During my testimony I described how in one church I visited, crutches, canes and walkers were nailed to the wall as "evidence of healing." Then I presented my wig to be nailed to one of the church walls so that when people saw it they would be reminded that "in Jesus' name the blind shall see, the lame will walk, the deaf shall hear [and in Jesus' name the bald shall 'flip their wigs']."

So I left my wig there that day. I no longer need it; my thick, brown hair now grows so quickly it needs cutting often. Almost every time I look in the mirror I am reminded that God is faithful in freeing us from bondage when we are open and honest and obedient.

As I rejoice over Tina's new freedom, I am constantly amazed at the ripple effect of honesty. Facing the truth about myself and speaking it to others has been an important factor in freeing me from my compulsions. That my openness and candor could affect others like Tina excites me, of course, but it also reminds me all over again that the real power is from God. The more open and honest I am, the more He can do His work through me.

-*17* -

Letting the Tiger Out

$\mathscr{R}$ECOVERY $\mathscr{P}$RINCIPLE # *17*
Like Yourself

$\mathscr{F}$ood issues, I am discovering, are the most prevalent, persistent addiction problems with women. With men, too, but to a lesser degree. Women have a particularly emotional relationship with food. To us food can be a source of immense pleasure or intense pain. It can be comforter, accuser, faithful lover, enemy to be avoided.

Women live in a society in which they are judged by their exteriors. Losing weight can somehow assume ultimate importance, a way of waiting for life to happen: "Once I lose weight. . . ." All of life would be better, happier, more rewarding if only we were thin.

If and when all of us foodaholics manage to become thin, we find to our dismay that the anticipated paradise is a glittering sham perpetrated enthusiastically and profitably by Madison Avenue. The media has blitzed us with images of skinny models in diaphanous dresses sipping white wine on windswept beaches while slender men with perfect teeth nibble on their ears—the glorification of the body beautiful. If we but have one, all is well.

Not too long ago I went on a doctor's controversial diet, losing 25% of my body weight—about 40 pounds. Whoever said, "You can't be too thin,'' was wrong. I carried the diet to a compulsive extreme, starving myself in the process. My anorexic mindset was taking over again.

There was a lot of ego in my dropping several dress sizes, but the gaunt wisp I became hardly had the energy to pick up a Kleenex. I had little flesh. My breasts shrank. My eyeballs gaped like burnt holes in a blanket. To my alarmed husband I aged a decade in eight months. But I had ribs for a change and hip bones and a teeny waist.

I was not suddenly transformed into the devastatingly alluring creature I thought I would be if only I could lose those stubborn twenty pounds or so. Nor was I happier or more fulfilled. My problems did not suddenly vanish when I became thin. The mystique of skinny is just that—a mystique.

I found that some women resented my being thin. Heavier was better, less threatening to others. I would be asked, ''What size are you now? A two?'' These women were starving themselves on lettuce leaves and cottage cheese or liquid diets. Somehow they thought I had arrived at dieter's nirvana, that golden circle of wonderfulness where all is well.

It is a lie perpetrated by the multibillion dollar diet industry.

I went off that diet and got onto a sensible, more nourishing eating program. Now I am back at the insurance company's chart of ideal weight for my height, although it is a struggle to stay there as I crave the sugary, yeasty foods I shouldn't have. (''I don't need a cookie. There's always celery!'')

Part of this new program is to allow myself two special treats weekly. A piece of pie . . . a divine cheese croissant . . . a dish of frozen yogurt. Otherwise I would go off the deep end.

In my recovery from addictions, while dealing mostly with overweight, I have discovered that the way to maturity where food is concerned is being aware of behavior patterns and feelings that have kept me in bondage to my need to overeat (and undereat). Mostly I was stuffing down my feelings—guilt, fear, anger, boredom, frustration.

Eventually I learned to check on my feelings when my tummy

started rumbling. Exactly what was I trying to feed? Was it some psychological hunger (I'm eating because I'm scared of this situation)? Or was I *really* hungry?

Once I was able to spot-check my feelings, I could grab hold of that Scripture handle that has been so helpful to me in checking compulsions in general: "Take every thought captive to the obedience of Christ."

Freedom has come as I become more aware of who I am and how I use food to cope with stress, anger, rejection, shame. I feel a new kind of euphoria knowing I can now make choices, life-giving choices, that I don't need to be chained to old patterns.

For me, a journey to the past was necessary to understand why food gave me so many problems. For me as a child, as for so many, food represented security and love. Food was a reward, too. Mom baked a lot. There was always some fresh-baked love offering waiting for me when I got home from school: warm peanut butter cookies, ginger-snaps or my favorite, chocolate chip.

"You've worked hard today at school; you deserve a special treat" was the message. Good girls got rewards, so I always worked hard to be not just good but *p-e-r-f-e-c-t!*

Since I was an only child, my mother hovered over my food intake, often insisting I eat her portion as well as my own, especially meat—a precious commodity in our meager budget. I remember how Mother would cut out the best part of her pork chop for me, content to chew on the fat and bone. Her sacrifice made me uncomfortable. Sometimes my tummy balked at swallowing what I felt should have been my mother's nourishment, that somehow I was taking what she needed.

We parents use food as a punishment, too. I think back with horror how I forced my firstborn, Brad, to sit in his high chair for over an hour until he cleaned his plate of the seven remaining garden peas. Finally, in desperation, he ate one and mashed the other six in his hair.

Have you ever noticed how angry people eat? They stab their food as if they expect it to attack them back. My Uncle Ralph used to eat that way, impaling each bite as though it were his mortal enemy.

I have watched anorexics eat—or not eat. I was one myself at one point. Food is merely rearranged on the plate, very little of it finding its way to the mouth. Meat is cut into tiny pieces and slipped under lettuce leaves. A nibbled roll lies nearby looking as though a mouse has chewed on it. It seems to the anorexic as though she has eaten a full meal.

At the other extreme are those (more typical of my own food abuse) who almost become human garbage pails. When most dysfunctional, I could all but inhale a two-pound box of chocolates. Another binge for me was a fresh-baked loaf of bread slathered with butter and peanut butter. My midnight raids into chocolate ice cream were hour-long orgies.

Chocolate was my smooth, undemanding, sensual friend. It lulled me. It seduced me. It satiated me—temporarily. The next night I would crawl back for more, coming to hate myself for my weakness. Indeed, a love/hate ambivalence has always characterized my response to food. It was my nurturer, my mother, my betrayer, my subtle poisoner. No wonder my weight ballooned upward of 200 pounds!

My shopping cart was a telltale giveaway. Chips, cookies, six-packs of beer, cartons of Twinkies and candy bars. Peanut M & Ms were utterly irresistible.

Once while standing in line at the neighborhood market checkout, I heard two women discussing me, thinking I was out of earshot.

"Doesn't she ever look at herself in the mirror?" one of them was saying.

To which the other replied, "Sad, isn't it, for someone who's been in the Miss America pageant to let herself go to seed the way she has. She couldn't win a cattle contest now!"

Those words should have seared themselves with white-hot pain into my heart and brain. But I shrugged them off, refusing to believe I looked as awful as I really did. My view of myself was most myopic— just what I saw in my hand mirror when I put on my makeup.

As my life turned around and I began to deal with my compulsive behavior, the first two enemies I confronted were alcohol and tobacco. Eventually, with God's help, I stopped drinking and smoking. Food, however, was hard to class as an enemy. After all, everyone has to eat.

At an eating disorder support group meeting I attended once, some-one put it this way: "The alcoholics have it easy. They simply learn to put the cork in the bottle and keep it there. We food junkies have a tiger in the cage. Three times a day we have to let it out, feed it, pet it, make friends with it and then put it back in its cage."

The moment of truth came when I was looking for a dress to wear for my fortieth birthday celebration. In a three-way fitting room mirror I saw myself in full-length 3-D and couldn't believe the mass of flesh I had become. My upper arms looked like Smithfield hams, while bulges and rolls of fat creased my midsection. Heartsick, I ambled up to the cash register to purchase the only dress I could find that would fit: a dreadful black-and-rust print voile number with long sleeves and an elastic waist. It made me look like an overstuffed chair. I consoled myself on the way home with a triple-dip pecan and pralines ice cream cone.

At treatment centers and then later at the halfway house, I managed to bring my weight down from the 200 area to about 160. By the time I married Len I had droppped to around 150. Yet still I had not dealt with my food issues. I was still eating compulsively, then dieting compulsively.

Now that I am on a strict physician-prescribed eating program, I realize how often food has become that special treat I felt I deserved. After all, my codependent, people-pleasing self needed a fix when she took on the cares of the world. What better gift than something de-lectable to eat! I could space out. Medicate. Forget for a moment what feelings and problems were plaguing me.

Now my special treat to myself when I feel tempted to pig out is to take a few minutes to work on a crafts project, phone a friend, write a letter. One of my favorite treats: propping up lots of pillows on my bed and reading a news magazine. That is loving myself without involving food.

A recent incident during a family gathering at the farm tested my new food discipline. I knew that on top of the refrigerator sat a blue-berry pie. Not some plastic bake-it-yourself frozen variety, but the *real thing*, a confection baked at a local Virginia dispensary of epicurean delights, Hill High Orchards.

Hill High pies are the ultimate treat for our family. People request them on birthdays. Some of us have been known to drive miles out of our way for Hill High pies. You're talking gourmet here.

This particular evening I happened to be returning from an errand to nearby Leesburg, Virginia. I knew the family planned to have that blueberry pie for dessert. It would be warmed in the oven, slathered with heavenly French vanilla ice cream and accompanied by piping hot chocolate raspberry coffee—none of which my food plan allowed.

But I didn't have to sit there and watch, drooling. I could have a special treat of my own. With sudden inner decision-making intensity, I wheeled my car into the parking lot of a supermarket.

Seizing a grocery cart, I marched determinedly to the vegetable counter. The produce manager was misting his offerings. The tiny droplets did make them look a bit more appetizing lying there glistening seductively . . . if a beet can look seductive!

But not just any veggie would do. It had to be special. If I couldn't have blueberry pie, I would have an artichoke.

My exploring fingers plunged into the artichoke bin. After careful testing, I laid a pale green trophy lovingly into my grocery cart. It was gorgeous and I congratulated myself.

Chinese vegetables were next. I spent several minutes selecting the most perfect snow peas I could find. No blemishes. No spots. No splits. Perfect snow peas.

My heart leaped as I saw fresh parsnips smiling at me from little plastic bags. Parsnips excite me. My mouth was already watering as I fantasized a steaming plate of sweet parsnips dotted with my permitted small portion of butter.

At the far end of the counter, a siren vegetable sang a tantalizing song. Imported yellow peppers from Holland . . . $4.99 a pound. Should I?

"Why not?" I argued back.

I found the most lusciously tempting golden pepper in the bin, lifted it to my lips and gave it an enthusiastic kiss. Anyone watching me

166

would have thought I had really lost it! Fortunately the produce manager had finished his misting duties. I was alone.

My spirits were soaring as my car purred down the winding road to Evergreen Farm. It was a dazzling night. The trees and fields were ablaze with thousands of tiny blinking lights from early summer fireflies.

What a fairyland! I thought to myself. *How could I get so wrapped up in a pie with all this beauty around? Forget the stupid pie. I have a bag full of perfect snow peas.*

During our evening meal I savored my special veggies for the benefit of the pie-eaters, although I have to admit I did have a few secret yearnings to join them. But I am working on it, trying to reprogram myself.

Like most Americans I have been bewildered by the variety of diets screaming at me from television ads and headline stories in magazines at supermarket checkouts. What to believe? After extensive research, plus some sad experience with diets that take weight off but offer no formula for keeping it off, I have come up with ten general suggestions:

1) Find a food plan that is comfortable for you over the long term, allowing you special treats every now and then.
2) Cut down on portions at each meal, saying no to seconds.
3) Limit consumption of sugar, salt, bread, baked goods, junk foods. Eat less red meat, more fish and chicken.
4) Drink six to eight glasses of water every day.
5) Exercise five days each week. Daily, if possible. Brisk walking works for me.
6) If you are severely overweight, see a physician for a medical checkup and ask him or her for a food plan.

7) Don't put your life on hold waiting to be thin.

8) Combine disciplined eating and exercise with a spiritual plan that emphasizes quiet times, prayer, Scripture reading.

9) If you are struggling with a food problem, it is crucial that you attend a support group.

10) Remember, God loves you as you are. As one person put it at a support group meeting, "I can accept myself as I am because God has shown me I'm no less of a person in His eyes, in spite of the big numbers I put on the scale."

– 18 –

Learning to Say I'm Sorry

RECOVERY PRINCIPLE # 18
Confess Your Wrongdoing

$\mathscr{H}$e looked frail and gaunt in his favorite chair, a rose-beige recliner. His calloused hands and stained fingernails told the story of years of long labor—repairing, renovating, refurbishing. Dad was one of those men who could fix most everything.

In my youth he and I had spent many hot summer days papering and painting the houses we lived in. I am grateful to him for helping me acquire so many home repair skills.

"I've always been the son you never had, Dad," I would tease as I climbed a ladder bearing a long strip of pasted wallpaper or a brush loaded with paint. He would always make sure his foot was planted securely on the lowest step of the ladder so it wouldn't fall over.

My heart was warmed now by the memory of that long-ago protective gesture.

"You're doing a fine job!" he would say.

Those were golden words of high praise from my father. His exacting eye and penchant for detail seldom missed a thing. How I wanted to please him, to do my very best!

We hung miles of wallpaper and spread a pond of paint in those days together. They were precious times of work and fellowship, times I needed to remember after he divorced Mother and moved out of our lives into a new one of his own. How angry I had been then!

That was forty years ago. Now I was sitting opposite him in the living room of his home in Barre, Vermont. My stepmother, Nora, had gone "downstreet"—a New Englandism for the shopping district— and I welcomed this time to be alone with him.

As I sat looking into his lined face, I thought back to the movie-star-handsome father of my youth. He was still attractive now and virile despite his siege of illnesses. His smile was warm and loving. His new false teeth seemed fashioned for a much larger face, giving him the appearance of being all teeth. His weary blue eyes shone with love for his only child.

Secretly I had always wondered what it would have been like to have had brothers and sisters. How would my life have been different? Would these siblings now be supportive to my parents as they grow older and the attendant infirmities set in? I felt very alone. Yet I had a special helper.

My mind flashed over to the guest house where Len and I were staying during our visit here. He had been poring over a manuscript, his black-rimmed half-glasses perched on the end of his slender nose. Looking up as I left the room, he had shot me a reassuring look.

"Call me if you need me."

Those words came back to comfort me as I sat in the silence of my father's living room. Len was there for me, whatever lay ahead with my parents. He was the brother I never had; he was friend, counselor, teacher, lover, all in one.

The late afternoon sun filtered through the sheer white curtains, highlighting my father's wispy gray hair. His skin was pale, splotched with red patches from his fever. Dark age spots dotted his forehead and hands and peppered his scalp. I bit my bottom lip in an attempt to keep from crying. He suddenly looked so vulnerable and helpless.

Perhaps he sensed my discomfort. He broke the silence.

"I just want you to know how much it means to Nora and me to have you and Leonard here. It seems there is never time enough. . . ." He dropped his eyes to the toes of his quilted brown leather slippers.

I jumped in. "Daddy, I only wish we lived closer, that our separations didn't have to be so long." I felt tears rising again. The lump in my throat ached like a stubbed toe.

"I guess I need to ask you if you have any fears right now, Daddy. Is there anything you're worrying about that we could talk about?"

I felt awkward asking these questions.

"No, honey, there isn't anything in particular that I can think of. With the house paid off and no other major debts, I'd have to say things are O.K. When I get to feeling better, I'm going to get to the lawn outside with my weed-whacker."

Dad was doing what he always did—avoiding talking about feelings. I eased back in my chair, resigned to his changing the subject, knowing that we could never explore together a troubling concern on my heart: that before I was born my father had been so unhappy in his marriage that he had not looked forward to being a father. I had long since forgiven him for this. But how to show it?

Suddenly he looked me straight in the eye. "Honey, I'm worried about you. That I'm not doing enough for you."

Was this the confession of a man who felt remorse over his divorce and my subsequent alcoholism? Or a father's present concern for a very busy daughter?

His blue eyes filled with tears. He managed an embarrassed cough to cover the depth of his emotions.

I moved quickly to his side, kneeling before him on the floor in front of his chair. "Oh, Daddy, don't be worried about me. I'm happy and fulfilled!"

I took his strong, rough hands in my own. Before I knew it we were embracing. His strong, wiry arms around me held me close. The roughness of his gray cardigan chafed my cheek in the gusto of the embrace.

"Daddy, I'm so sorry for everything I've done that has hurt you. Please don't blame yourself for what happened to me. I made some very foolish decisions in my life. It's not your fault that I became an alcoholic."

I sobbed into his shoulder, my hand tracing the sharp outline of his protruding shoulder blade beneath the sweater. He was fragile, a far cry from the robust man I had embraced so often in the past.

"Dad," I continued, "this may seem silly, but I want you to repeat after me: I am not responsible for Sandra's alcoholism. I am *not* responsible for Sandra's alcoholism."

Haltingly and self-consciously, he repeated the sentence twice, then smiled wanly at me as though he didn't really believe what he had just said.

His voice cracked again and his face crumbled in some long-held grief. "I'm sorry, too, dear, for everything that has happened. I hope you will forgive me, too. I love you."

"Oh, Daddy, I love you, too," I repeated, flooded with a great sense of relief. We hugged and swayed in our embrace.

My legs smarted with little prickles from the uncomfortable position. It didn't matter. I felt a new sense of freedom, of forgiveness and reconciliation with my father. I had waited many years for this moment.

Only the night before, when I was speaking with my mother on the telephone, she had broken down and said almost the same words: "I'm so sorry for what happened. I wasn't there for you in high school."

How well I recognized the guilty anguish in her voice. Not having been there for my own children in high school, I knew only too well how parents agonize over their children's addictions and pain, convinced somehow they are responsible.

"Mom," I said tenderly, "you aren't to blame for what happened to me. You really aren't. Can you understand and believe that?"

Silence at the other end of the phone.

"Mother, please repeat after me: I am not responsible for Sandra's alcoholism."

She laughed nervously. "I don't know if I can say that."

I insisted, making her repeat the sentence twice after me.

A pause, then a nervous chuckle of relief. Mom was working her way toward freedom, too.

My parents' marriage ended when I was sixteen. Dad moved out the night before my senior year began at Spaulding High School.

It was a difficult year. Not just "What am I going to be when I grow up?" or "Am I making the right career decision?" but feeling the burden of meeting my mother's burgeoning emotional needs now that Dad was gone.

At first I decided to enroll in the dental hygiene course at the University of Vermont. Yet when I entered my family dentist's office for a routine exam, the heavy medicinal aroma assaulted my nostrils with reality: This was not at all what I wanted to do.

Since I was a child I had loved to draw and paint and create crafts projects. Somewhere deep down inside, I had nurtured a dream of attending art school. So after deciding not to be a dental hygienist, I applied to the Rhode Island School of Design and, to my astonishment, was accepted.

This caused a major flap between my divorced parents. Dad thought I should not abandon the University of Vermont course, which he felt would lead to something practical for me; Mother favored art school. I went to art school.

I was nineteen when Dad remarried in 1955. Mother did so in 1961. Both second marriages were happy and fulfilling. But, as with most divorces, bitterness and resentment remained.

Ironically, it was the downturn in my life years later that resulted in their reconciliation. As I sank into alcoholism and life-threatening depressions, my parents had to communicate about the darkening situation of their one child. Soon parents and stepparents started having meals and get-togethers.

My father and stepmother were especially attentive to Mom during my stepfather's hospitalizations, leg amputations and death in 1983. They became an important part of my mother's support system.

After my session alone with Dad, I knew I had unfinished business with him and my stepmother regarding a bitter root judgment I had made against them years ago. When Dad married Nora, I vowed to myself that I would never forgive them. Over the years I made many more inner vows concerning men: Men were not to be trusted. They would let you down when you needed them. They would wind up hurting you. These all-but-forgotten oaths rotted away at my soul.

One night we were all three seated in their living room about to watch a Saturday night comedy show, when I asked Dad if he would mind turning off the television. There was something I had to say.

Dad and Nora both looked a bit startled, but switched off the TV, settled deeper into their recliners and fixed concerned stares on my face. I shifted uncomfortably on the sofa and dug my shoes into the soft carpet.

"It may seem to you that I've completely recovered from my alcoholism, that I'm now normal. Well, I'm not sure what normal is today. They say that 96% of all homes are dysfunctional in some way or another."

I paused, struggling for the right words.

"For years I covered up my deepest feelings. It was always important for me to put up a good front. Often I didn't even know what my real feelings were.

"But I was devastated when you left us, Daddy. I was angry at you. Mother fell apart and I felt totally responsible for her. She was so fragile and I became—well, like her mother. I felt so trapped and confused. Even though I threw myself into school and after-school activities, part of me was always with her, wondering if she was all right, wondering how she would be when I got home from school.

"Usually I found her in the same place—sitting on the footstool by the telephone, the curtain drawn back with one hand, her anxious, sad face peering out the window waiting for a glimpse of me coming up the street.

"The curtain would whish back into place as soon as she saw me, and she would be at the door to welcome me, smiling with her lips, her eyes hollow and haunted. She was such a fragile little bird. I wanted to make up to her what she had lost.

"I knocked myself out trying to be there for her, but what does a sixteen-year-old know about being a parent? Or a spouse?

"I blamed you, Dad, even though I knew it wasn't all your fault. I knew from the time I was a little child that you and Mother weren't suited for each other. I tried so hard to make the difference. To keep your marriage from collapsing. I tried to be everything you both wanted me to be. And somewhere along the way I got lost in the process. I am still finding out who I am today.

"I blamed you, too, Nora, for what happened, maybe wrongly. And I hardened my heart toward you both. Even though I was cordial on the outside, part of me on the inside reared up and said, 'I'll never forgive you for what you've done to Mother and me.'

"But over the years this unforgiveness has been a weight on my heart. I've known I needed to deal with it. So I'm asking you to forgive me for my judgment of you. I am truly sorry. Can you forgive me?"

After a stunned pause, Dad spoke first. "Well, of course, honey, I forgive you. Gee whiz, I never knew you felt that way. . . .''

His calloused hands picked at the fabric on the arms of his chair.

Nora broke the silence. "I didn't know you felt that way either, Sandra. But I've always loved you and thought of you as a daughter. . . .''

Then Dad started talking about how the house needed painting. Nora commented on the rainy weather. I realized how uncomfortable it was for us all to talk about our feelings.

"If we could," I continued nervously, "let's get back to the subject at hand. I just want you to know that I love you both, and I want to thank you for standing by me and loving me when I wasn't lovable. For supporting me with your prayers. I am truly sorry for everything I've put you through."

I was starting to cry now. "Could I give you both a hug?"

They both stood up and all three of us joined in a hug. After much nose-blowing and wiping of eyes, the television blinked on.

My mind was not on the program. I closed my eyes, stretched out on the couch and fell asleep—a peaceful, blessed sleep freed from a long, dark shadow of the past.

Steps eight and nine of the twelve-step program of Alcoholics Anonymous stress the importance of making amends to those people "we have harmed.'' This is always difficult, sometimes impossible, because of circumstances.

Making amends, of course, often includes saying, "I'm sorry." Here again, many of us falter. The words we know we should say stick in our mouths.

"Why is this?" I have often asked myself. "Is my pride blocking the words?"

Pride, yes. Fear of showing weakness, too. Sometimes guilt freezes the words inside us. I have struggled with all of this.

What has helped me overcome these blocks is my daily times with the Lord. During these times I not only pray but listen to what He has to say to me. So often have I felt His love, His forgiveness, that it was easy to say, "I'm sorry, Lord, for making such a mess of my life. I'm sorry, Lord, for failing to keep Your commandments. I'm sorry, Lord, for all those years I wasn't a good wife and mother, daughter, friend. . . .''

Saying "I'm sorry" to the Lord this way has made it much easier to say "I'm sorry" to the people I have hurt.

More recently I have been able to say the following twelve healing words that can completely restore a relationship:

I am sorry.
I was wrong.
Please forgive me.
I love you.

During that same visit to Vermont, my mother and I were invited to dinner at Dad and Nora's. After the meal we settled into the music room—Nora at her bench before the small spinet organ, Dad in an old oak rocker to my left and Mother on his other side.

The tones of the organ filled the air with light melody. "When I grow too old to dream, I'll have you to remember. . . .''

Out of the corner of my eye, I witnessed a beautiful little vignette of forgiveness and reconciliation: Dad's hand, so thin from recent illness, rested on one arm of the rocker. For just a moment, Mother's small, arthritic hand moved from her lap and touched my father's hand ever

so lightly, patting it gently. Then her hand disappeared back into her lap.

Being allowed to view this tender moment in that little window of time did a healing work in me.

Because so many of us have family relationships that need healing, I now use the following prayer for forgiveness in my talks and seminars, adapted from one I heard Brennan Manning use at a Life in the Spirit seminar:

> Lord Jesus, I ask You into my heart.
>
> Please touch those life experiences of mine that need to be healed.
>
> Since You know me so much better than I know myself, bring Your love to every corner of my heart. Wherever You discover inner wounds, touch me . . . console me . . . release me.
>
> Walk back through my life right now to the very moment in which I was conceived. Cleanse my bloodlines, Lord. Bless and

protect me as I was being formed in my mother's womb. Grant in me a deep desire to be born. Heal any traumas that could have harmed me during the birth process.

Thank You, Lord, for being there to receive me into Your arms at the very moment of my birth, to welcome me onto the earth, to assure me that You would never fail me or desert me.

Jesus, please surround my infancy with Your light and Your love. If my earthly family failed to meet my physical or emotional or spiritual needs, supply them now from Your infinite store. Give me renewed confidence and courage to face the trials of the world because I know my Father's love will support me even if I stumble and fall.

Lord, by the power of Your Spirit, empower me to forgive myself for my past failures, for any hurts I may have inflicted on others, for my mistakes, for my moments of weakness and selfishness.

Lord, I give myself to You body, mind and spirit, and I thank You for making me whole. My gift to You this day is to radiate Your Spirit of forgiveness, Your Spirit of love, Your Spirit of joy as I reach out to serve others for You.

-19-

Wounded in the Womb

People with low self-worth who are struggling to free themselves from addictions to drugs, food, tobacco, *et al.* are pursuing a new avenue of help these days—therapy for *in utero* wounding. Counselors are discovering that clients who fail to respond to regular techniques often improve when the stress and trauma of the time in their mothers' womb is probed.

John and Paula Sandford, well-known Christian authors and counselors, find that many of their clients experience major breakthroughs in healing when they are "prayed through" the rejection and abandonment that happened *before* birth. Thomas Verny, M.D., in his book *The Secret Life of the Unborn Child* (published by Dell in 1982 and still in print), discovered that the mother's and father's behavior toward the unborn child has major impact on the child's mental health and sense of well-being.

The moment a smoking mother thinks about lighting up a cigarette, the child in her womb will wriggle in anticipation; the little one is already addicted to nicotine that has entered its body through the placenta. News reports are full of articles and pictures of crack babies born from mothers on drugs.

My friend Dawn suffered for years from feelings of shame and low self-worth. When we prayed about this one day, she revealed to me that her father never knew who his father was, and that when drunk her father would scream out that he was a bastard, an accident, a heap of manure that nobody wanted. No wonder Dawn had no sense of her own value!

Dawn had also been a victim of abuse while in the womb. She told me tearfully that her father used to beat her mother during the pregnancy, hitting her and kicking her in the stomach. "I don't want you or this damned kid," he would bellow as he pummeled them both.

As Dawn grew up and learned of her mother's trauma during the pregnancy, she felt guilty that she had been such a terrible burden. She tried to take care of her mother, a frail, sickly, bedridden woman who gave birth to four more children after Dawn.

As Dawn became the surrogate mother of the brood, she was also the victim of an incestuous relationship with her father. As the oldest functional female in the home, she was expected to cooperate when her father wanted sex. She soon learned that he wouldn't beat her mother or siblings if she cooperated.

"I knew I was the child of a bastard," she told me. "My father drummed this constantly into my head. But he didn't need to. I already felt I was a mistake and worthless."

Dawn went on to tell me that she had received counseling and therapy for traumatic memories of incest, domestic violence and guilt toward her mother. She felt there had been some healing.

I sensed the Lord saying Dawn needed specific prayer for a healing of those experiences she had suffered in the womb. When we went back to her *in utero* experience she began to sob; then she gagged and choked and retched and whined like a whipped, helpless puppy.

I held her and in my prayer told her, "Dawn, you are loved and cherished and precious in the sight of God. You are a blessing, not a burden."

Her body gave a little shudder and then relaxed. As I ended the prayer, she was limp in my arms; then her teary eyes opened and a radiant smile crinkled her thin face. Some long-held burden had been lifted. A key had been given Dawn to unlock a dark room her memory had never been able to enter.

"Don't let Satan rob you of what has just happened," I advised her. "He'll try to steal your joy, your healing, and whisper doubts and judgments to you. But don't listen. He's a liar. Thank God every day for your healing and believe you have been healed, because you have."

Then I gave her an assignment. "Today I want you to do something that is childlike. I want you to get in touch with the little girl Dawn who never was able to play. Life has been serious for you from the time of your birth. I want you to give yourself permission to play."

Dawn looked doubtful. "I'm not sure I know how to do what you're asking. My mother always told me that play was a foolish waste of time. That's going to be a tough message to erase, but I'll try."

My experience with Dawn brought back a flood of memories of my own pregnancies. All three came in a 36-month period. I was unprepared emotionally, physically and spiritually to be a mother even of one. Two lively toddlers were already taking every ounce of my resources when the obstetrician gave me his stunning announcement: "You're pregnant."

"I can't be pregnant again," I gasped.

I was already in a downward spiral of addiction, and my marriage was in deep trouble. I felt trapped. Frantic. It wasn't right to bring another life into this troubled situation! I went from the doctor's office to my car and sat helplessly in the driver's seat, then pounded my stomach in desperation. A pathetic attempt to abort?

In the weeks and months that followed I raged mentally at the unborn child. Somehow the message must have been conveyed from my thoughts to the embryo in my body. Starting in the sixth month, the small life inside me tried to abort every day at twelve noon. It apparently found the womb a hostile place. Soon I was bedridden. And Lisa was born sensing she was not wanted.

As I learned more and more about *in utero* wounding of the fetus,

I wept bitter tears over that time in my life. How could I make amends to Lisa? To help her know she was valued and loved?

During Lisa's first visit to Evergreen Farm after I began asking myself these questions, I felt a consuming desire to pray with her. To rock her. To go back in time and speak to that unborn child, little Lisa in the womb.

On the face of it, impossible! She was 27 years old. Yet I had learned we can go back and pray through traumatic situations in the distant past. I had received deeply powerful healings myself in this area.

Would Lisa think it was crazy or weird? Was it appropriate even to try? Would it turn her off?

The night before her visit was to end, I felt the time was right. Lisa and I had just spent several days in Charleston, West Virginia, visiting relatives, allowing us many hours together in the car. I had welcomed this opportunity to have her undivided attention. We had time to dig in on some painful issues.

The last leg of the seven-hour drive back to Virginia had been especially poignant. I had talked with her about my alcoholism and how it had robbed me of my ability to be a nurturing mother. We had wept together as the miles rolled by. I felt a new bond with my beautiful adult daughter. We were friends, more peers than mother and daughter. But always little Lisa was just below the surface. So many fears and insecurities. So much pain buried under years and years of denial.

We had finished dinner and she was in her room packing. I joined her there. The room was a clutter of bags and suitcases and girl things. The nudge to *Do it now* could not be ignored. "Lisa," I said hesitantly, "I'd like to pray for you in a way that may seem rather unusual. I'd like to just hold you and rock you and pray for healing deep inside you when you were damaged in the womb."

I felt frightened and vulnerable, but knew I needed to press on. Lisa looked startled.

"Would that be all right with you?" I continued. "Could we do it now before you have to leave?"

"Sure, Mom, that would be O.K."

Her willingness, guarded as it was, encouraged me that God was carving out this special time for us.

We struggled somewhat awkwardly to get our bodies into a comfortable position. I sat on the side of the bed and she placed her head against my chest, her arms around my waist, her long legs extended along the bedspread. We shifted our weight self-consciously, laughing nervously.

"Pretty tough to rock without a rocking chair, isn't it?" I laughed.

"No, Mom, this is fine."

I could feel Lisa's slim body relaxing in my arms. I smoothed her long hair away from her forehead and gently kissed the top of her head, her hair fragrant and flower-fresh.

How beautiful this precious child is, I thought. *How could I ever have considered aborting her? How horrible that would have been.*

Our bodies rocked together slowly. Forward and back. Forward and back. Lisa tightened her grip around my waist and snuggled her head closer to my chest.

As we rocked I gazed out through the sheer white Priscilla bedroom curtains to the verdant panorama of Evergreen Farm in the twilight. The bushes and trees and hedges rose from the lawn like hundreds of green guardian angels.

How safe I felt in this setting, my child nestled on my breast. Healing was happening without a word being spoken.

Finally I broke the silence. "Lisa, I want to speak to little Lisa in the womb, to hold her and rock her and reassure her of some things.

"Little Lisa, I need to tell you that I am filled with such joy that you are in my womb. You are wanted very deeply. You are precious and lovely. Feel the comfort and warmth of my love as you grow. You are treasured. I love you so much.

"I speak life and blessing and health and freedom to your little spirit and I thank God that He has given you to me as His incredible gift of love and trust.

"I welcome you onto the earth as your mother. How blessed I am

that you are my little girl! For you are 'fearfully and wonderfully made.' Welcome, little one! Welcome.''

Then I asked Lisa's forgiveness for neglecting her needs as a little girl, for being insensitive and selfish, for abandoning her to the care of babysitters while I pursued my own selfish interests. For all the hours she was left alone, waiting for me to come home. My "I'll be home in just a little while" meant hours and hours.

By now I was sobbing and so was she.

"Oh, Lisa, please forgive me. I only wish I could roll back the clock and have another chance to be the mom I could have been if I hadn't been a drunk.''

"It's O.K., Mom," she whispered. "It's O.K. I always knew you loved me. It's O.K.'' I offered her a tissue and dabbed at her nose and snuggled closer. Neither one of us wanted this moment to end. We rocked some more.

Then, as we broke from the embrace, an astonishing ending. Suddenly I was aware of brilliant light all about my daughter. If the sun had not gone down, it could have been sunbeams through the window. I felt suffused in the glow of this light—warmed, bathed. Then it faded.

We both blinked and smiled and broke into girlish laughter.

But that wasn't all. The room was filled with the fragrance of lily of the valley. And neither us was wearing perfume.

The next afternoon when Len and I drove her to Dulles Airport for her trip back to Montana, Lisa had a glowing smile on her face. She was radiant as she walked down the corridor to her plane. She walked proud and tall, with a new set to her shoulders. She had been affirmed. She knew she was loved, that she was precious. A weight laid on her in the womb had been lifted.

The "you are loved" affirmation contains great healing power. Receiving it from God washes me clean every day. Hearing it from others is balm to my spirit; it nourishes me, frees me from resentments and irritation, feeds my soul.

When I say it to others, I can see their eyes light up, tense faces soften, bodies relax. These three words are a form of therapy—not only to those who receive it, but for me, too, as the source. I can never say the words without feeling a warmth inside; yes, even an exhilaration and spirit-to-spirit connection to my God above and to the person I care about.

The healing that Lisa and I experienced at Evergreen Farm was a milestone in our mother-daughter relationship, but only one step on a long journey. There is always farther to go in this healing process.

Another get-together took place in Vermont when Lisa and I visited there in May 1991 to be with my father, who had gone through major surgery at the age of eighty. We stayed with Mother in her small Montpelier home and took daily trips to Barre to visit Dad and Nora.

One morning I awoke to a symphony outside Lisa's and my window as a flock of birds trilled their joyous alarm-clock greetings. I inhaled deeply the moist air, fragrant with lilac and honeysuckle. Nearby Lisa's beautiful face seemed almost angelic in the morning light, her long, chestnut hair cascading over her pillow.

What a treasure she is, I thought to myself. *Thank You, Lord, for such a precious gift.*

Unconsciously I extended my right hand close to her, resting it a few inches from her slumbering face. Suddenly she reached over for my hand and grasped it firmly with hers—like a little child reaching out in sleep for its mother's touch.

Lisa's breathing never changed, her eyelids never flickered. Before my eyes, her sleeping face took on a cherubic expression as this 29-year-old was transformed into a very little girl holding her mother's hand. Her face held such contentment! Peace. Trust.

Deep within my spirit I sensed healing happening to me as well, as though the Lord was doing a cleansing and restoring work in my heart. He knew my anguish for all the times I had failed Brad, Brent and Lisa during their infancy and growing-up years. I had been too self-absorbed and ill to be a real caring mother to them. I had asked both God and them to forgive me, but self-forgiveness was elusive.

I found myself praying, *O Lord, reach deep within Lisa's memory. Use this moment as our hands are clasped to heal those innermost hurts she carries—all the times she reached for me and I wasn't there for her.*

Then I prayed for myself. *Lord, please forgive me for all the times I neglected Lisa and Brad and Brent. Use this moment to wash away the guilt and pain and condemnation I can't seem to let go of.*

The tears were running down my cheeks, splashing onto the cool, white sheets.

I'm so tired of feeling guilty. I know You don't want me to feel this way. My head knows that, but my heart doesn't seem to. Please make it a reality.

Lisa's grasp relaxed a bit, but still she hung on. Such a bonding! I felt God's love in every fiber of my being. The room radiated it. And the birds outside rejoiced with us.

Lisa let go of my hand and rolled over.

I believe we had both been touched and transformed in mysterious ways we will never understand.

- *20* -

I Blew Them All Kisses

---

*R*ECOVERY *P*RINCIPLE # *20*
Reach Out

---

*A*s I write these words I am suddenly aware that the recovery process in my life has been going on now for almost fourteen years. It began in August 1978 when I met Karen at the Montana State Hospital and she spoke to me of a Person whose name I didn't want to hear: Jesus. Yet I discovered over time that there was *hope for the hopeless* through that name.

The recovery road still stretches ahead of me for an indeterminate stretch. But the slowness of the process does not discourage me. On the contrary, the process itself has been so enriching, the experiences I have had so edifying, that in some strange and hard-to-understand way I am far ahead of where I would be without all the heartache and tragedy.

The farther I travel, the stronger is my faith. Though excruciatingly difficult at times, the journey has been exhilarating, with many stimulating people met along the way. So much pain at times. But pain, I have discovered, is a necessary part of the journey.

Most of all, the journey has been an adventure. It became an adventure the moment I let go of my life and surrendered it to God.

"I've made a mess of it," I confessed. "Will You be in charge from now on?"

Being out of control is difficult for me, and there are times I try to take over and run my life as I used to. Thank You, Lord, for not letting me get away with that! For with Him in charge I have made wonderful new friends, have had a loving and fulfilling marriage, discovered gifts I never knew I had (like putting words together on paper), traveled to places I never dreamed I would see.

And the adventure goes on. . . .

I am astonished at how rapidly my healing continues when I *reach out* to help others.

Soon after my marriage to Len a recurring thought began to nag at me. The idea persisted. But it wasn't until June 1991, about a month after my healing experience with Lisa at Mother's house in Vermont, that I mentioned it to him casually.

"What do you think about my going out to see Eve?"

He looked at me in surprise. Then his face creased in thought.

"Why not?" he said slowly. "Your visit might give her a real lift."

Though Len's first marriage had been painful, his visit to Eve in the nursing home in 1989 had been surprisingly upbeat. Len, Eve and their daughter, Linda, had prayed together for a healing of all the hurts of the past.

But now I began to have mixed feelings about traveling all the way to Iowa to see Len's first wife. She might resent me and my role with Len and the three children she bore. It could be painful for me, too. Not just the encounter itself, but here I was going into another institution and reliving all those old emotions of being shut in because of my illness.

Yet I was continuing to learn to obey that inner voice. It had directed me into other difficult situations that had ended up aiding my recovery.

Eve and I had at least one thing in common: We were both dealing with the need for self-forgiveness.

Furthermore, as a recovering alcoholic myself, perhaps I could relate to Eve in a way no one else could.

When I called Linda for her reaction, she not only liked the idea but suggested that she and her daughter Mary Catherine, age six, go, too, since Eve had never seen her granddaughter. A great idea from my beautiful step-daughter! We chose a weekend that month.

The three of us met at the Des Moines International Airport and drove together to the nursing home in Albia.

When we walked into Eve's room, the stunning beauty of the former *Vogue* model was hauntingly apparent in her ashen face. Her large, warm brown eyes jumped to life as she saw us. Mary Catherine offered her a handmade paper Easter basket, which she had carried all the way from the airport in Washington, D.C.

Eve accepted this gift of love in her arthritic hands and held it tenderly. In a deep contralto voice choked with emotion she said, "My granddaughter made this for me?"

I was saddened to see this once vivacious soul, now bent and twisted, imprisoned in a wheelchair. There was a fragile birdlike quality about her—a tiny Dresden doll almost too delicate to touch.

During our weekend visit Eve stretched herself beyond her frailties, her earthbound restraints. Her spirit was buoyant. She thanked us over and over for coming to visit her. Several times she said to me, "Sandy, I feel like I've known you all my life."

I took that as a wonderful compliment, glad she felt comfortable with me, that she liked me. It was important to me to have the love and approval of the mother of Len's children.

Saturday evening was a special occasion, when we had dinner at a popular restaurant. As I looked at the three faces around the table I thought, *What an incredible happening!* This was the evening of June 22, 1991—the sixth anniversary of my marriage to Len, who was on this day giving a speech at a Presbyterian conference in Branson, Missouri. I was celebrating our anniversary with his first wife, their daughter, Linda, and his granddaughter, Mary Catherine, named after his second wife.

God, how amazing You are! I thought as I buttered my dinner roll. *You are in the business of bringing broken families together in ways no one could ever imagine.*

189

Eve asked me to please cut up her chicken breast, and added, "I really like you, Sandy. You're just like an old shoe."

Sunday morning we wheeled Eve into the Methodist church. At one point during the Sunday service I glanced over at her to see how she was getting along. Her doll-like frame was silhouetted against a large stained glass window. In the center section, Christ was pictured with His hand outstretched, a small white lamb nestled peacefully against His chest. In her white suit Eve looked somewhat like that little white lamb—small and fragile and vulnerable. I sensed that Jesus had also reached out for Eve and drawn her to His bosom.

The enormity of her loss struck me: three children relinquished to other mothers, five grandchildren she hardly knew, a life of missed opportunities.

The stark reality: I could just as well be the one in that wheelchair!

The high point of the weekend was our prayer time. The four of us held hands, three of us praying aloud for each other, with Mary Catherine's participation powerfully sweet in its silence. Then Eve and I were alone while Linda and Mary Catherine prepared for the drive to the airport.

"Is there anything else we should pray for?" I asked.

Then the thought came: "Eve, I feel we both know God has forgiven us, but have we been able to forgive ourselves?"

The look of pain on her face stabbed me. With tears streaming down her face, Eve asked God to help her forgive herself. I prayed the same prayer.

Later, as Linda, Mary Catherine and I drove to the airport, I made a discovery. I had gone to Iowa thinking that in some way I might be of help to Eve. Perhaps I had. But what came through strongly was how she had ministered to me. As her spirit bonded with mine, and as we prayed together for self-forgiveness, something had broken inside me. The barrier preventing me from truly forgiving myself was continuing to dissolve.

My recovery continues. Today I see myself as the not-so-compulsive woman. Yet I am staggered some days by the depth of woundedness inside me; layers and layers keep emerging to be dealt with.

On an occasion just recently the principle of reaching out collided with my inner fear of institutional confinement. After I spoke to a women's group one night in a coastal city in Florida, a gray-haired woman in her mid-sixties approached me. Bright brown eyes snapped beneath bushy salt-and-pepper eyebrows.

"I'm a social worker," she said, introducing herself. "Is there any way you could come and speak to my girls?"

Betty's girls, it turned out, were inmates in a correctional facility. Something pricked my heart. I remembered only too well what it was like to be locked up in an institution. I remembered with gratitude the dedicated people from the outside who cared enough to come and teach or bring music.

I said yes.

"Would you be able to come tomorrow morning?" she pressed.

"I guess so," I replied, taken back at the immediacy of her request.

I had some difficulty finding the facility, a low sandstone building in a remote section of town. Inside the front door stood a beaming Betty. Her cheeriness warmed my weary self. It had been a short night with little rest after a long evening of speaking and talking to people.

Inside the somber building, the sameness of institutional sights and smells hit me—disinfectant and floor wax and stale cigarette smoke. A shudder of thankfulness surged through me. *Thank You, God, that I am free of these places!*

Beyond the reception area was a glassed-in booth where an officious woman guard spoke to us through a small hole in the glass.

"Sign in, please," she said briskly, sizing me up through half-closed eyes.

In spite of my visitor status, the attitude of this young guard triggered feelings in me of helplessness and guilt from the past.

She's just doing her job, I reminded myself.

Betty clipped on her staff badge. "I'll lock Mrs. LeSourd's purse up in my closet," she told the woman in the booth. "But Sandy, you'll have to leave your car keys here." I pushed my keys under a small opening at the bottom of the glass cage.

Betty strode ahead down the hall, introducing me to colleagues

191

along the way—the staff nurse in a white pantsuit, another nurse in a tailored gray suit.

Betty showed me her office, which she shared with the program director, an enormous black man named Lester. He pumped my hand enthusiastically, a gold front tooth glistening from his smile like a beacon light.

"Thank you so much for coming," he said. "Would you mind if some of the boys came to hear you, too?"

This was hardly what I expected.

"If they don't mind, I don't," I replied weakly, trying not to show my mounting panic. What in the world did I have to say to young men in a detention ward?

The cafeteria was a large room filled with fifteen or more round white tables, plus colorful plastic chairs—blue, red and orange. A large plate glass window looked out onto a grassy courtyard. To the left was the kitchen where an industrial-strength dishwasher chugged loudly. *Will anyone be able to hear me over that noise?*

My eyes turned to the double doors as the inmates entered slowly. Five young black women ranging from 16 to 25, I guessed. They eyed me suspiciously, then slumped into chairs around a corner table.

Then the invasion of young men. Some looked to be in their teens, others in their early twenties. Dressed in navy regulation uniforms, they looked as enthusiastic as convicts en route to a firing squad.

As they filled up five or six tables, I was aware of scores of eyes sizing me up. Self-consciously I smoothed the pleats of my white cotton skirt and adjusted my knotted silk belt. *Am I overdressed?*

A tough-looking teenager in a Mohawk haircut caught my eye. He shot me a surly glance, then closed his eyes and pretended to sleep. A curly-haired boy perhaps sixteen smiled weakly, his puppy dog gaze strangely affirming. He seemed to be the only one even vaguely interested in my presence. The rest of the group wiggled and squirmed in the hard plastic chairs; some rested their heads on the tables.

Suddenly I felt very tender toward them.

"Mrs. LeSourd has come to be with us today to speak with you about her experiences," Lester said. "She is a former Miss Vermont."

This was met with stony indifference.

I began by telling them how I had been locked up in an institution for many months. Mild interest.

Then I told of being sexually abused at age five, and gave statistics on the number of boys and girls molested before age eighteen. Knowing looks, downcast eyes. The pain and shame in the room were palpable.

I told them of people praying for me while I was so ill in the institutions and "I believe these prayers changed my life." Shrugs.

Betty, who had heard my talk the night before, chirped, "Sandy, tell them about Karen."

"Yes. Karen. I met her when I was in the Montana State Hospital. What a wreck I was!" I told them how I sat around chainsmoking cigarettes, locked up as a hopeless alcoholic and prescription drug addict, when this new patient arrived. She kept talking about Jesus and I tried to avoid her but couldn't. She was beautiful in an almost ethereal way.

"One night," I went on, "Karen came into my room, sobbing her heart out. She kept asking me if Jesus loved her. I got out of bed and held her in my arms and told her, 'Yes, Jesus loves you.' "

I went on to describe how something happened to me as I did that. "For a moment I stopped thinking only about myself and was concerned about someone else. And with that I began to get well.

"Strange thing, though. Karen left the hospital as suddenly as she arrived. I never had a chance to talk with her again."

Some interest.

"Years later I wanted to send a book to Karen. So I wrote to the Montana State Hospital asking for Karen's address. Guess what the hospital wrote back?"

Of the whole group, only Mohawk was not listening. His eyes were still closed.

"They had no record of Karen's ever being in that institution."

My young audience waited silently, expectantly.

"Does anyone here know why they had no record of Karen?"

The heads were all shaking *no*.

"It's my conviction that Karen was an angel, that God loved me so much—as He loves every one of you—that He sent an angel to rescue me."

Surprised looks. Expressions like "Wow!" and "Way to go!" Lester was grinning ear-to-ear. Mohawk opened his eyes for the first time.

"I believe each of you has a guardian angel," I continued. "And I hope you believe that, too."

One or two heads nodded. Others looked as though it was news too good to be true, at least for them. Undoubtedly many felt God had abandoned them or double-crossed them by giving them uncaring parents or no parents at all.

An announcement crackled over the public address system, my cue to stop. The exodus from the cafeteria began. The girls lined up and marched out first. The youngest smiled shyly at me in thanks.

I BLEW THEM ALL KISSES···

The boys touched my heart. As they lined up to leave, I got several smiles. One young teenager with a thatch of honey-colored hair looked at me with moist eyes, his lips quivering. I could feel his spirit leap out to me in pain and desperation, and I wanted to hug him and take him home with me.

As I walked down the hall I stopped briefly outside the boys' ward. A huge pane of gray glass separated me from them. I looked more closely. There was Mohawk. He was grinning. One of the boys waved at me. I waved back. Several others shot me the ''V for victory'' sign. I did the same. Mohawk and the others were now on their feet hopping up and down and waving at me.

Then I waved my arms as if they were angel wings. I must have looked pretty stupid to anyone who had not just heard the Karen story! But the boys loved it. Again I flapped my wings. They waved wildly.

Then I blew them all kisses. They blew kisses back.

My heart was full to bursting as I walked out of the building to my car.

RECOVERY PRINCIPLES

\# 1 *Seek Prayers of Others*

\# 2 *Say No*

\# 3 *Trust God's Love for You*

\# 4 *Accept Yourself*

\# 5 *Smell the Flowers*

\# 6 *Obey the Inner Voice*

\# 7 *Give Yourself Away*

\# 8 *Be Vulnerable*

\# 9 *Be Reconciled*

\#10 *Identify Your Real Needs*

\#11 *Expect the Best*

\#12 *Seize the Moment*

\#13 *Forgive Those Who Have Hurt You*

\#14 *Talk About It*

\#15 *Celebrate*

\#16 *Be Honest*

\#17 *Like Yourself*

\#18 *Confess Your Wrongdoing*

\#19 *You Are Loved! Believe It*

\#20 *Reach Out*

When You Need Help . . .

Here are addresses and telephone numbers of some of the programs available

1) Alcohol Addiction

Alcoholics Anonymous
P.O. Box 454
Grand Central Station
New York, NY 10017
(212) 686-1100

Alcoholics For Christ, Inc.
1316 North Campbell Rd.
Royal Oak, MI 48067
1-800-441-7877

Alcoholics Victorious
National Headquarters
P.O. Box 10364
Tigard, OR 97210
(503) 245-9629

ACA
Adult Children of Alcoholics
P.O. Box 3216
2522 W. Sepulveda Blvd., Suite
    200
Torrance, CA 90505
(213) 534-1815

Al-Anon Family Group Hdq., Inc.
P.O. Box 862
Midtown Station
New York, NY 10018
(212) 302-7240

2) Codependency

Co-Dependents Anonymous, Inc.
P.O. Box 33577
Phoenix, AZ 85067-3577
(602) 277-7991

3) Child Abuse

Child Help USA
P.O. Box 630
Hollywood, CA 90028
(213) 465-4016

National Child Abuse Hotline
1-800-422-4453

4) Cults

International Cult Education
   Program
P.O. Box 1232, Gracie Station
New York, NY 10028
(212) 439-1550

Spiritual Counterfeits Project
P.O. Box 4308
Berkeley, CA 94705
(415) 540-0300

Shield of Faith Ministries
(Recovery from cult, occult or New
   Age experiences)
Sharon D. Hilderbrant, M.A.
P.O. Box 19367
Denver, CO 80219

5) Drugs

Cocaine Anonymous
World Service Office
3740 Overland Ave., Suite G
Los Angeles, California 90034
(213) 559-5833
1-800-347-8998 (meeting referrals)

Cocaine Hot Line
1-800-COCAINE

Drugs Anonymous
P.O. Box 473
Ansonia Station
New York, NY 10023
(212) 874-0700

Marijuana Anonymous
1527 North Washington Ave.
Scranton, PA 18509

Nac-Anon (Family Group)
P.O. Box 2562
Palos Verdes, CA 90274
(213) 547-5800

Narcotics Anonymous
P.O. Box 9999
Van Nuys, CA 91409
(818) 780-3951

The National Clearinghouse for
Alcohol and Drug Information
P.O. Box 2345
Rockville, MD 20852
(301) 468-2600

National Drug Abuse Information
and Referral Line
1-800-662-4357

National Federation of Parents for
Drug-Free Youth
1423 N. Jefferson
Springfield, MO 65802
(414) 836-3709

Substance Abusers Victorious
One Cascade Plaza
Akron, OH 44308

6) Eating Disorders

BASH—Bulimia Anorexia
Self-Help, Inc.
1035 Bellevue Ave., Suite 104
St. Louis, MO 63117
(314) 567-4080 or (314) 991-BASH

Eating Disorders Hotline
1-800-382-2832 (U.S.)
(212) 222-2832 (NY)

Overeaters Anonymous
P.O. Box 92870
Los Angeles, CA 90009
(213) 542-8363

O-Anon
General Service Office
P.O. Box 4350
San Pedro, CA 90731

National Assoc. for Anorexia and
  Associated Disorders
Box 271
Highland Park, IL 60035
(312) 831-3438

7) Emotional Disorders

Emotions Anonymous
International Services
PO Box 4245
St. Paul, MN 55104
(612) 647-9712

Recovery, Inc.
The Association of Nervous and
  Former Mental Patients
802 North Dearborn St.
Chicago, IL 60610
(312) 337-5661

8) Compulsive Gambling

Gamblers Anonymous
P.O. Box 17173
Los Angeles, CA 90017
(213) 386-8789

Gam-Anon/Gamateen
International Service Office, Inc.
P.O. Box 157
Whitestone, NY 11357
(718) 352-1671

The National Council on
  Compulsive Gambling, Inc.
445 West 59th St.
New York, NY 10019
1-800-522-4700

9) Homosexual Issues

Exodus International
(For homosexuals and their
    families; also for sexual
    addiction)
P.O. Box 2121
San Raphael, CA 94912
(415) 454-1017

Spatula Ministries
(Parents of homosexuals and
    children with AIDS) Barbara
    Johnson, founder/director
P.O. Box 444
La Habra, CA 90631
(213) 691-7369

10) Incest

Incest Survivors Anonymous
P.O. Box 5613
Long Beach, CA 90805-0613
(213) 428-5599
National Domestic Violence
    Hotline: 1-800-333-7233

Survivors United Network
Kempe Foundation
3801 Martin Luther King Blvd.
Denver, CO 80205
1-800-456-HOPE

VOICES in Action, Inc.
(Victims Of Incest Can Emerge
    Survivors)
P.O. Box 148309
Chicago, IL 60614
(312) 327-1500

11) Intervention

For an intervention specialist, write:
    Families in Crisis, Inc.
    7151 Metro Blvd.
    #225, Edina, MN 55435
    (612) 893-1883
    or contact local support groups or
    health professionals for further
    information in your area.

201

12) Obsessive-Compulsive Disorder

The OCD Foundation
P.O. Box 9573
New Haven, CT 06535
(203) 772-0565

13) Sex Addiction

Sex Addicts Anonymous
P.O. Box 3038
Minneapolis, MN 55403
(612) 339-0217

Sex and Love Addicts Anonymous
Augustine Fellowship
P.O. Box 119, Newtown Branch
Boston, MA 02258
(617) 332-1845

Sexaholics Anonymous
P.O. Box 300
Simi Valley, CA 93062
(805) 581-3343

Co-SA
Codependents of Sex Addicts
P.O. Box 14537
Minneapolis, MN 55414
(612) 537-6904

S-Anon International Family Group
P.O. Box 5117
Sherman Oaks, CA 91413
(818) 990-6901

14) Sexual Abuse

Eleutheros
1298 Minnesota Ave., Suite D
Winter Park, FL 32789
(407) 629-5770

Free to Care Ministries
Jan Frank, Director
P.O. Box 1491
Placentia, CA 92670

The Recovery Partnership
Dale Ryan, Executive Director
P.O. Box 1095
Whittier, CA 90603
(213) 947-2685

Kempe Foundation
3801 Martin Luther King Blvd.
Denver, CO 80205
1-800-456-HOPE

15) Shopping/Spending

Debtors Anonymous Hotline:
(212) 969-0710

Debtors Anonymous
General Service Board
P.O. Box 20322
New York, NY 10025-9992

16) Smoking

The American Cancer Society
19th W. 56th St.
New York, NY 10019
(212) 382-2169

Smokenders
18551 Von Karman Ave.
Irvine, GA 92715
1-800-828-HELP

Smokers Anonymous World
  Services
2118 Greenwich St.
San Francisco, CA 94123
(415) 922-8575

Quit and Stay Quit
Terry A. Rustin, M.D.
9731 Greenwillow
Houston, TX 77096
(713) 728-4473

17) Suicide

For information write:
American Association of
  Suicidology
2459 S. Ash
Denver, CO 80222

National Suicide Assistance
  24-Hour Hotline
1-800-333-4444

For information on the workshop:
  "Suicide—The Preventable
  Tragedy" contact:
John Hipple, Ph.D.
North Texas State University
Denton, TX 27603
(817) 565-2741

18) Workaholism

Workaholics Anonymous
Westchester Community College
AAB
75 Grasslands Rd.
Valhalla, NY 10595
(914) 347-3620

19) Other

Post-Abortion Recovery

WEBA
(Women Exploited By Abortion)
Kathy Walker, Director
3553-B N. Perris Blvd., Suite 4
Perris, CA 92370
(714) 657-0334

Post Abortion Counseling Services
Glenda Cervantez
P.O. Box 1134
Billings, MT 59103
(406) 245-6441

Families Anonymous, Inc.
P.O. Box 528
Van Nuys, CA 91408
(818) 989-7841
For those with a concern about the
use of mind-altering substances
or related behavioral problems in
a relative or friend

Recovering Couples Anonymous
P.O. Box 27617
Golden Valley, MN 55442
For couples in recovery together
with the desire to remain in a
committed relationship

The Spiritual Dimensions in
Victims Services
(for victims of all types of crimes)
David W. Delaplane, executive
director
P.O. Box 163304
Sacramento, CA 95816
(916) 446-7202

Ministry to Singles

The Tear Catchers
Harold Ivan Smith
P.O. Box 24688
Kansas City, MO 64131
(816) 444-5301

20) Treatment Centers

For information about the location of more than 1,600 centers offering various programs and services for recovery write:

Rapha—Christ-centered in-hospital counseling care units, treating psychiatric, substance abuse and other addiction problems for the Chrisian community. Has numerous locations nationwide.

Rapha
Box 580355
Houston, TX 77258
Nationwide number 1-800-227-2657
In Texas 1-800-445-2657

Hope Community
Located in Culpeper, Va.,
with other facilities opening
  nationwide.
1-800-333-HOPE

U.S. Journal National Treatment Directory
Customer Services
320 S.W. 15th St.
Deerfield Beach, FL 33442
1-800-851-9100

Minirth-Meier Clinic—Comprehensive mental health care services, substance abuse, eating disorders and other addiction treatment. Numerous locations nationwide.

Minirth-Meier Clinic
P.O. Box 1925
Richardson, TX 75085
1-800-232-9462

Ephesians 5:18 Life Ministries
16819 New Hampshire Ave.
Silver Spring, MD 20904
(301) 424-9713

21) Other Helps:

Hazelden Educational Materials
Box 11
Center City, MN 55012
1-800-328-9000

Tools for Recovery
Recovery Publications, Inc.
1201 Knoxville St.
San Diego, CA 92110-0832
(619) 275-1350

U.S. Journal, Inc.
1721 Blount Rd., Suite 1
Pompano Beach, FL 33069
1-800-851-9100

Johnson Institute
7205 Ohms Ln.
Minneapolis, MN 55439-2159
(612) 831-1630

Compcare Publications
2415 Annapolis Ln.
Minneapolis, MN 55441
1-800-328-3330

Lifeworks Communications
20300 Excelsior Blvd.
Minneapolis, MN 55331
(612) 475-4911

If you want more comprehensive
information (self-assessment
tests, suggested readings, etc.) on
the compulsive-addiction
problem, I refer you to my first
book, *The Compulsive Woman*
(Chosen Books, 120 White Plains
Rd., Tarrytown, NY 10591).